## Praise for *Deligl*

*Delighting in Jesus* is like a cool breeze on
dened by the pace of this world, Asheri
easy yoke. I have long believed we see (
joys He gives us, and this book will teach you how to open your eyes. by embracing a daily life of delight in God, we find a truly joy-filled existence.

**Phylicia Masonheimer**
Founder & CEO, Every Woman a Theologian

Tired? Broken? Bored? You've come to the right place. This book is filled with profound biblical truth that is perfectly balanced with practical, creative applications for rediscovering your delight in Jesus. If you've lost your sparkle, invite a group of friends to rediscover their spiritual wonder, joy, and satisfaction as they learn to practice spiritual rhythms that will change their lives. Asheritah Ciuciu is a name you will remember. This is an important book.

**Carol Kent**
Executive Director of Speak Up Ministries, speaker, and author, *He Holds My Hand: Experiencing God's Presence and Protection*

Jesus captivated the imagination of my heart. He filled me with light that drove all of my ideals, a fullness of heart and truth upon which to make my daily decisions. Asheritah has captured that beauty and strength that Jesus brings as He offers us His life in exchange for ours. I know the message of this book will breathe a fresh understanding of His reality, His love, and His presence into the lives of all who read it.

**Sally Clarkson**
Bestselling author of over thirty books

There comes a point in our walk with the Lord when the Bible fails to inspire, our prayers seem to go nowhere, and God feels unreachable. Where do you go when you hit a crisis greater than your faith? This book answers that question. Reading through it, you will experience Asheritah as your encourager, a guide who knows the road out of discouragement and into renewed delight in the Lord.

**Juli Slattery**
President and cofounder of Authentic Intimacy

If you've hit a spiritual wall, found yourself staggering through a desert of the soul, grieving a crushed dream, or reeling from a fallout of faith, take heart—you have found just the right book. In these pages, Asheritah Ciuciu will lead you to the fountain of joy, springing from the Father's heart for you. *Delighting in Jesus* is biblically deep yet wide with wonder, compassionate yet clear, realistic in naming the struggles of today yet rooted in our Christian heritage.

**Aaron Damiani**
Lead Pastor, Immanuel Anglican Church

If there's anyone I trust with a message about the complicated emotion of joy, it's Asheritah Ciuciu. She's been tested and tried, and yet her life testifies to the joy we can find through Jesus, no matter what we face. I can assure you: this book isn't a book of platitudes, happy bows, and cliches. This is a book that grapples with all the nuances of joy, diving you deep into the Scriptures to find the answers you long for and pairing that with practical rhythms to restore your joy. For anyone who asks, "Where has my joy gone, and will I ever get it back?," this is the book you've been waiting for.

**Jennifer Dukes Lee**
Author of *Growing Slow* and *It's All Under Control*

With beautiful and gut-wrenching authenticity, Asheritah Ciuciu helps guide us back to our pure delight. Like a dear friend grabbing our hand and helping us find our way back to the path in the pitch dark, this book is full of wisdom, encouragement, and just the right amount of nudging to get our steps on track. It's not one-size-fits-all. There's no secret code. But I found myself memorizing the rhythms and using them day in and day out as it all pointed me back to *the* Source. Jesus. What a powerful and life-changing read!

**Kimberley Woodhouse**
Bestselling author of more than forty books

With refreshing vulnerability, Asheritah meets her readers in the brokenness of life where joy is often missing, having been inexplicably lost or stolen away by a multitude of enemies. And then she reminds us through God's Word that we were designed by Christ for just the opposite. You are sure to find great encouragement as you walk with her to seek the pulse of life in Jesus that leads to joy fulfilled.

**Mike Castelli**
Lead Pastor, The Chapel Green

A pervasive system of religion has robbed us of the abundant life and relationship Jesus intended for us to have with Him. Asheritah, with her gentle confidence in God's goodness, breaks us free from stifling misconceptions about God and leads us back to a path less traveled. *Delighting in Jesus* captures our imagination for what God always intended. It's an invitation to see God as He is and walk with Him in renewed joy.

**Karl Clauson**
Pastor of 180 Chicago Church, host of *Karl & Crew*, and author of
*The 7 Resolutions: Where Self-Help Ends and God's Power Begins*

# DELIGHTING in JESUS

Rhythms to Restore Joy
When You Feel Burdened,
Broken, or Burned-Out

## ASHERITAH CIUCIU

MOODY PUBLISHERS
CHICAGO

All Scripture quotations, unless otherwise indicated, are taken from the Holy Bible, New International Version®, NIV® Copyright ©1973, 1978, 1984, 2011 by Biblica, Inc. Used by permission of Zondervan. All rights reserved worldwide. www.zondervan.com The "NIV" and "New International Version" are trademarks registered in the United States Patent and Trademark Office by Biblica, Inc.™

Scripture quotations marked csb are taken from the Christian Standard Bible®, Copyright © 2017 by Holman Bible Publishers. Used by permission. Christian Standard Bible® and CSB® are federally registered trademarks of Holman Bible Publishers.

Scripture quotations marked (NLT) are taken from the Holy Bible, New Living Translation, copyright ©1996, 2004, 2015 by Tyndale House Foundation. Used by permission of Tyndale House Publishers, Carol Stream, Illinois 60188. All rights reserved.

Scripture quotations marked (ESV) are from the ESV® Bible (The Holy Bible, English Standard Version®), © 2001 by Crossway, a publishing ministry of Good News Publishers. Used by permission. All rights reserved. The ESV text may not be quoted in any publication made available to the public by a Creative Commons license. The ESV may not be translated in whole or in part into any other language.

Scripture quotations marked (LEB) are from the Lexham English Bible. Copyright 2012 Logos Bible Software. Lexham is a registered trademark of Logos Bible Software.

Scripture quotations marked NKJV taken from the New King James Version®. Copyright © 1982 by Thomas Nelson. Used by permission. All rights reserved.

Published in association with Jenni Burke of Illuminate Literary Agency, www.illuminateliterary.com.

All emphasis in Scripture has been added.

Edited by Amanda Cleary Eastep
Interior and cover design: Brittany Schrock
Cover concrete texture copyright © 2024 vectonauta/Freepik. All rights reserved.
Author photo: Ashley McComb Productions

Library of Congress Cataloging-in-Publication Data

Names: Ciuciu, Asheritah, author.
Title: Delighting in Jesus : rhythms to restore joy when you feel burdened, broken, or burned-out / Asheritah Ciuciu.
Description: Chicago : Moody Publishers, [2024] | Includes bibliographical references. | Summary: "Lift your gaze from your to-do list and get to know the One who knows you by name. Discover the theological foundation for how we were Created for Delight, consider three Robbers of Delight, and learn five practical Rhythms of Delight. Discover joy-filled freedom to connecting with God"-- Provided by publisher.
Identifiers: LCCN 2024028589 (print) | LCCN 2024028590 (ebook) | ISBN 9780802419507 | ISBN 9780802498120 (ebook)
Subjects: LCSH: Joy--Religious aspects--Christianity. | Jesus Christ--Devotional literature. | Christian life. | BISAC: RELIGION / Christian Living / Spiritual Growth | RELIGION / Christian Living / Women's Interests
Classification: LCC BV4647.J68 C528 2024 (print) | LCC BV4647.J68 (ebook) | DDC 241/.4--dc23/eng/20240719
LC record available at https://lccn.loc.gov/2024028589
LC ebook record available at https://lccn.loc.gov/2024028590

Originally delivered by fleets of horse-drawn wagons, the affordable paperbacks from D. L. Moody's publishing house resourced the church and served everyday people. Now, after more than 125 years of publishing and ministry, Moody Publishers' mission remains the same—even if our delivery systems have changed a bit. For more information on other books (and resources) created from a biblical perspective, go to www.moodypublishers.com or write to:

Moody Publishers
820 N. LaSalle Boulevard
Chicago, IL 60610

1 3 5 7 9 10 8 6 4 2

*Printed in the United States of America*

To the Shepherd of our souls:
never once have You left our sides,
never once have we walked alone,
but always
Your goodness and mercy have guided us
—into green pastures and by still waters—
that we would dwell in Your presence forever.

We can't wait to see You face-to-face,
the One we love,
the One we yearn for,
the One we live and move and have our being for.

Your bride is making herself ready for You.
Come, Lord Jesus. Come.

# Contents

# As We Begin

M y pen scratched against the paper as I jotted down the words:

> Turn and answer me, O Lᴏʀᴅ my God!
> Restore the sparkle to my eyes, or I will die. (Psalm 13:3 ɴʟᴛ)

Dramatic much? Sure.

But as I wrote the verse in my notebook, copying it word for word from the screen at the front of the conference room, I'd never felt more seen in my life.

And if David could be dramatic when praying, then surely the Almighty wouldn't mind a bit of drama from me. After all, He'd included this psalm in the Scriptures, and at that moment, it felt like this verse had been preserved throughout the ages just for me.

The conference speaker's voice faded into the background as I looked up the verse in its context, thinking that David would couch the drama in a bit more logic. But no. If anything, I felt he had put words to the heaviness I'd been carrying around for months:

> O Lᴏʀᴅ, how long will you forget me? Forever?
> How long will you look the other way?
> How long must I struggle with anguish in my soul,
> with sorrow in my heart every day? . . .

Turn and answer me, O Lᴏʀᴅ my God!
Restore the sparkle to my eyes, or I will die. (Psalm 13:1–3 ɴʟᴛ)

Restore the sparkle, Lord. I feel like I'm dying inside.

## Where Was My Joy?

Guilt flooded my soul as heat rushed to my cheeks. After all, what did I have to complain about?

Objectively, I had everything my once teenage self could have hoped for, and so much more: I'd married my high school sweetheart, we were raising our three beautiful children in a lovely neighborhood close to both sets of grandparents, and I was living my childhood dream of writing and speaking, training thousands of people around the world to find joy in Jesus through creative Bible habits.

So why was I unhappy?

Why did I want to quit everything and become a florist or a barista—anything that didn't resemble my current occupation?

Why did the quiet cry of desperation knock inside my rib cage, screaming to be let out?

Where had all my joy gone?

And more importantly: How would I get it back?

## Asking for Help

I didn't know the answer to that question, but I knew I needed help. So, the next day, after the speaker finished her message on becoming a courageous leader, I waited for the room to clear before approaching her.

"Hi, um, you don't know me, but when you put that verse on the screen, the one about restoring the sparkle to your eyes . . . that was for me."

I stared at the lapel of her neon green blazer, not daring to lift my gaze for fear that she'd see me as the fraud I clearly was.

This woman of God was nearly half a century older than me, and for just as long, she had ministered as a writer and speaker. If anyone would understand, she would. I wasn't sure what I expected her to do, but I hoped someone more experienced could show me the way out of the darkness and despair.

She tilted her head to catch my eye, and I reluctantly looked up. Her smile was kind and the laugh lines around her eyes bore testament to laughter that seemed to follow her into every room she walked into. But it was her blue eyes that captivated me. I kid you not: they were sparkling.

## Don't Be Afraid of Being Broken

I wish I'd recorded our conversation. I wish I could go back in time and revisit that moment, to ponder every word Carol spoke over me. But all I have are a few scribbled notes I jotted immediately afterward, and the lingering sense that God Himself was speaking to me through His faithful servant.

"Don't be afraid of being broken," she said. "Of your own brokenness or being around others' brokenness. Jesus still heals today."

That was it. I lost the fight with tears as they poured down my cheeks, my mascara leaving obvious streaks. But I didn't care. I was standing on holy ground.

All the brokenness from the past decade—mine and those I loved—made my shoulders sag under the weight of the heavy burden: relational tensions, church hurt, parenting struggles, career exhaustion, parental abandonment, secret addiction, health challenges, and on and on. The busyness, the brokenness, the burden . . . it all felt too much. Even amid all the reasons I had to be grateful, sorrow still threatened to crush my soul.

"God has seen," her gentle voice continued. "And He has promised: 'My joy will be your strength.' God Himself will sustain you."

I sniffed to keep the snot from running down my lips. But if she was grossed out by my embarrassing display, she was too mature to show it.

"God will sustain you in the darkness," Carol repeated, "and His Word will be a lamp to your feet and a light to your path. But don't sprint ahead of Him. Stay close to His side. At the right time, He will show you the way to go. But for now, He wants you to meander the path with Him."

Meander the path with Him.

Was it possible that in this darkness, God desired to reveal Himself more personally to me? Could it be that the sorrow pressing down on my soul was not evidence of God's absence or His displeasure but rather His invitation to lean deeper into Him?

"In those parts where you feel broken," she concluded, "let the Lord be seen through You. And know, down to the marrow of your bones, that God will indeed restore the sparkle to your eyes. Faithful is He who called you, and He will do it."

That promise felt like a distant dream, but the fact that you're holding this book proves that God keeps His promises. Every time.

He has indeed restored the joy to my soul and the sparkle to my eyes. Those heavy burdens I carried into the room that day? They haven't magically disappeared, but they're no longer pressing into my back because Jesus is shouldering their weight.

Looking back on the path I've walked with Jesus to get here, I long to tell every weary soul along the way: God sees you, He knows you, and He longs to restore His joy in you.

## Radiating His Joy

Almost a year to the day after the conversation in that conference room, I stood outside another conference room, on the other side of the country, holding the hands of another woman.

This time, however, I was the speaker who had just finished giving a message, and the woman in front of me had tears brimming in her eyes: "When you described what God has been doing in your life, I knew I was in the right place," she said, swiping her sleeve across the corner of her eye. "Before I left for this retreat, I told my husband I'm coming to find my joy again. I know God is gonna to do it for me because He did it for you."

There I was, standing on sacred ground again. This time, I had the incredible privilege of being the one to proclaim the promises of God to another sister, to testify to the goodness of God, to remind her that His joy would be her strength even in the darkest moments. But ultimately, it was she who encouraged me most when she whispered to me at the end of our conversation: "When you speak about Jesus, your whole face lights up! You're radiating His joy, and nobody can fake that."

I'm simply awed by the kindness of God in my life: that He would care enough to listen to my cry of desperation—dramatic or not; that He would bend low, and scoop me up, and hold me close; that He would restore to me the joy of my salvation and the sparkle to my eyes, so that I might extend that same hope and invitation to others . . . it is a gift beyond expression.

Through the rhythms discussed in the book, God has taught me the meaning of the verse: "Weeping may stay for the night, but rejoicing comes in the morning" (Psalm 30:5). Like the inevitable rising of the sun on the horizon every morning, so too we move toward joy when we delight in Jesus. Though sorrow, pain, and suffering may come, we know who holds our future, and it's a bright promise indeed.

## At My Darkest, Jesus Felt Nearest

I won't say it made all those dark moments worth it because that cliché twists the real pain and sorrow we endure into some trite sentiment that fails to capture the complexity of our human experience. No, I wouldn't willfully walk through the agony of despair again just to write a book about it. I'm not a masochist. But I wouldn't trade the closeness and comforts of Jesus for a pain-free existence.

Truly, it was at my darkest that Jesus felt nearest. It was in my sorrow that the Man of Sorrows stood by me. It was in my wordless groanings that our High Priest interceded for me. It was in my aimless wanderings that my Good Shepherd sought me. It was in my defenselessness that the Lion of Judah roared His protection over me.

It was in that dark night of my soul that the theological truths I'd learned about Jesus as a little girl in Sunday school took on real flesh-and-blood meaning for me.

I wouldn't choose the darkness again, but I won't waste it either.

# If You've Picked Up This Book

If you've picked up this book, there's a very real chance that your own soul is crying out, "How long, O Lord? Turn and answer me. Restore the sparkle! I feel like I'm dying."

If you're weary or disheartened, this book is for you.

If you feel the crush of darkness closing in, this book is for you.

If you sense that longing for joy throbbing in your heart, this book is for you.

I can't promise you all the answers, but I do promise to share the rhythms God used to restore my joy as I've walked this path with Jesus.

What I offer instead is this humble invitation: *Come to Jesus.*

He's been waiting for you. Come all you who are thirsty, and drink from God's "river of delights." Come, all who are hungry, and "feast on the abundance of God's house," for He has prepared a table for you, and there's a place setting with your name on it.[1]

And I promise you that this book won't just be theory or theology: it's going to be profoundly practical to your life right away—not just on the good days but on your ordinary Tuesdays too. I encourage you to download the free Discovery Journal I've created to guide you through this process. You'll find space to take notes on what you're learning as well as reflection questions and response prompts to rediscover joy in Jesus as you read. You can download the Delighting in Jesus Discovery Journal at DelightingInJesus.com/book-resources.

Don't wait until you get your life together. It's precisely in our sadness and grief, in our brokenness and burnout, that God says, "Come."

Come and experience a loving God who delights in you!

---

1. See Psalm 36:8 and Psalm 23:5.

PART ONE

# Created for Delight

# CHAPTER 1

# Where Did All My Joy Go?

When did I become such a grumpy person?" I exclaimed, eyeing my friend over mugs of frothy coffee. We'd just parsed the most recent church scandal to hit the headlines, against the backdrop of growing tension in the American church over divided politics and post-pandemic policies. Like many young Christians in our generation, my friend and I were trying to make sense of realities unfolding around us.

"Oh, if *you're* grumpy, I don't know what that makes *me*." She stared me down with mock earnestness. "A curmudgeon, maybe?"

"Yes!" I smacked the table. "That's what we are. Curmudgeons." I nodded, and we sipped our drinks in silent companionship. After a few moments looking out the window, I turned back to her. "I don't want to be a curmudgeon anymore. It's so draining."

"It *is* tiring, isn't it?" she agreed. "Not just anyone can be cantankerous all the time. It takes a special kind of person to pull it off."

I grinned at her dry humor. "I mean, where do we go from here? If we're curmudgeons in our mid-thirties, what's left for us in our seventies and eighties?"

"We can figure it out as we go," she assured me, a glimmer in her eyes. "After all, we've hit rock bottom. The only place we can go from here is up."

## God Gives Me Happiness?

I hadn't always been grumpy. In fact, most of my childhood and into adolescence, people would remark that my face radiated joy, appropriately living into the meaning of my name: Asheritah.

It's one of the first questions I'm asked after introducing myself: "Oh, Asheritah. That's a beautiful name. Does it mean anything special?"

Indeed, it does.

I'll spare you the entire etymology, but the short story is that my father made up my name, which is why you've never heard it before. And while it's a tongue twister for baristas calling out my order—it's *Ash-er-ree-tah*, like margarita, in case you're wondering—I got to secure my own domain and social media handles, so there's that.

The Hebrew compound word means "God is my happiness" and can also be rendered "God gives me happiness," so I can't get away from this theme of joy even if I wanted to. It's a rich identifier that wraps itself around every cell of my being even as it's a signpost along every part of my story.

I imagine my mother rubbing her pregnant belly, a lonely twenty-one-year-old political refugee walking the gardens of a crisis pregnancy safe house in Athens, Greece, whispering my name as a blessing for both of us: God will be our happiness.[1]

I imagine my father speaking the name over me the first time he held me, three months after my birth, having just escaped communist Romania and reunited with us: God is still our happiness.

I imagine the confusion of my American preschool teachers, trying to pronounce my strange name when calling me in from recess, unknowingly calling out: God gives you happiness.

I can vaguely recall the quizzical looks of my aunt and uncle and great-grandmother when we first moved back to a newly freed Romania as missionaries, looks that seemed to question: God is your happiness?

I recall the good-natured teasing of my junior high classmates, testing shorter nicknames, while I'd insist they call me by my full name, Asheritah: God is your happiness.

I remember the first time my high school sweetheart tenderly said my name on the grassy banks of a river, promising himself to me forever: God gives me happiness.

People spoke blessing over my life each time they said my strange name, so how could I not grow up to live out that beautiful promise? Except, that happiness began to dim, and people stopped remarking on my luminescence. I began to wonder: If God truly was my happiness, where had all my joy gone? And how do I get it back?

I don't know you, but since you're reading this, there's a good chance you're wondering the same thing.

---

1. I've always been fascinated by the ancient practice of blessing one's children. Names carry great significance in the Bible, conveying not just identity but also a powerful trajectory for one's existence. This significance explains, in part, why God intervenes to change people's names at significant junctures in their lives, as with Abram, Sarai, Jacob, and Simon. I believe how we choose to name our children has far more significance than contemporary culture would have us believe, and we still hold the power to pronounce a blessing over our children and grandchildren.

## Remember Your Joy

Most of us enjoy at least some years of our childhood filled with a sense of wonder and delight. As children, we'd marvel at the puffy clouds floating outside our school window and imagine their shapes and the adventures they're drifting off to.

Remember losing yourself in the embrace of a furry friend, wrestling a puppy, or stroking the fur of a purring kitty?

Remember marveling at grown-ups' stories of epic adventures, hoping you'd grow up to experience the same?

Remember your childlike adoration of Jesus, caught up in the wonder of His love for the whole world?

Maybe you think back with fondness on the chocolate chip cookies your grandmother baked, the bike rides with your friends, or the sticky juice dripping down your chin at the annual watermelon eating competition. **Try to remember an early memory of absolute joy and delight: Where were you? Who were you with? What did that feel like?**

For some of us, that childlike delight stretches into our adolescence and early adulthood. And for some, the sense of wonder and joy leads into a naturally optimistic and joyful worldview.

Most of us, though, lost our joy somewhere along the way, whether suddenly (through a traumatic event) or gradually, as it wears out with age and the continual onslaught of global news, local community tension, and family fights. **As you reflect on your journey of joy, can you remember the last time you felt utterly enraptured right where you were?**

However long it's been, you've probably realized that delightful joy is hard to maintain on a daily basis because life offers plenty of hardships that steal our joy.

# Three Robbers of Delight

I wish there was a way to avoid suffering. If I could give you a three-step process to ensure that you and your loved ones never again experienced pain, I'd do it in a heartbeat. But there is no guarantee, because suffering is a part of living in this fallen world.

At times, we might feel as if someone is conspiring against us, as if they are out to steal our joy. The Bible tells us that Satan is a thief who "comes only to steal and kill and destroy" but that Jesus has "come that they may have life, and have it to the full" (John 10:10 NIV); and while that is true, sometimes our own decisions create circumstances that steal our joy. Sometimes, other people's choices and actions hurt us. But as we consider three common robbers of delight, remember that Jesus has come to restore what's been stolen and heal what's been broken:

> The Spirit of the Sovereign Lord is on me,
> because the Lord has anointed me
> to proclaim good news to the poor.
> He has sent me to bind up the brokenhearted,
> to proclaim freedom for the captives
> and release from darkness for the prisoners. (Isaiah 61:1)

Jesus is moving to undo the damage of sin in this world. As we survey these robbers of delight, I invite you to take a moment after each of these to reflect: Where have these robbers stolen your joy? And more importantly: how might Jesus long to move mightily in your life today?

## Burdens

We all carry hidden burdens, like we're pushing an invisible wheelbarrow of sorrows, failures, and regrets that grows heavier year after year. Our shoulders sag under the weight of unmet expectations, unrealized potential, and unresolved conflict.

Some of us carry the expectations of perfectionism, whether because of birth order, our workplace environment, or our own internal moral compass. Every misstep feels like a lump of coal added to the heap of failures in our wheelbarrow.

Others of us carry the burden of peacekeeping, navigating interpersonal conflict with perceived ease, but internally wrestling with the need to make sure that everyone else's needs are taken care of while our own energy wanes with the effort.

Some of us carry burdens of responsibility, like caring for elderly parents or special needs children, or just the regular demands of twenty-first-century life that seem to insist we perfectly balance a full-time job with regular exercise, nutritious eating, community involvement, and church volunteering.

And speaking of church culture, many of us carry the burden of trying to measure up to the unrealistic expectations of a "good Christian life": a daily quiet time, regular prayer hours, Scripture memorization, discipleship, evangelism, activism, hospitality, generosity, church attendance . . . are your shoulders sagging yet?

It's in a similar context of religious expectations that Jesus faced a crowd of people, weary and worn down by all they could not accomplish, that He says:

> "Come to me, all you who are weary and burdened, and I will give you rest. Take my yoke upon you and learn from me, for I am gentle and humble in heart, and you will find rest for your souls. For my yoke is easy and my burden is light."
> Matthew 11:28–30 (NIV)

Jesus invites those of us who are carrying heavy burdens to come to Him, to lay down our own burdens, and to receive His rest. The rest that Jesus offers us is the very first step of rediscovering joy because joy can only flourish in a heart that's at rest. Jesus removes the heavy burdens from our shoulders and leads us in "green pastures," making us "lie down beside quiet waters," so that He might "restore our souls" (see Psalm 23).

For me, this meant embracing rest for my body as well as my soul. After consulting with multiple medical providers and hearing the same advice over and over again, I finally got the message: I needed to sleep more, eat nutritious foods, pause for afternoon breaks, and take daily strolls outside. It turns out that we were not created to be machines that power through fatigue, illness, and sorrows as if they don't affect us. Rest—physically, spiritually, and mentally—is not only an act of worship, but also the first step toward healing.

Only after we've received His divine rest does Jesus call us to a new pace of life: walking in step with Him, shoulder to shoulder in His easy yoke, carrying a light burden. We'll unpack the full meaning of this passage and the beauty of Jesus' invitation in chapter 13, but for now, receive Jesus' invitation to lay down your burdens and slow yourself down to His unrushed cadence.

## Brokenness

The second robber of delight we may encounter is brokenness. Inevitably we'll get cut by the shards of this world fractured by sin and death, whether physical (injuries, disease, and addictions), emotional (loneliness, anger, and fear), or relational (marital struggles, friendship drama, and church hurt).

Some of us have been deeply hurt by those we were supposed to be able to trust. A deeply traumatic event casts its long shadows over the length of our days.

Some of us endure a thousand paper cuts from daily verbal jabs, leaving our hearts wounded and bleeding.

Some of us are physically hurt, our bodies deteriorating with age or disease, and every day we wake up wondering if we'll be able to function because of the chronic pain.

Some of us grieve the loss of loved ones whose days were cut too short. We feel broken, like we'd never be able to hold on to joy even if it were granted.

Thankfully, God doesn't ask us to fix ourselves before coming to Him. Instead, Jesus came "to bind up the brokenhearted," "to comfort all who mourn," and "to bestow on them a crown of beauty instead of ashes, *the oil of joy* instead of mourning."[2] Jesus is the ultimate Good Samaritan who binds up the wounds of the person beaten up and left for dead.[3] And to those who turned to broken cisterns for refreshment, Jesus calls out: "Let anyone who is thirsty *come to me and drink.* Whoever believes in me, as Scripture has said, rivers of living water will flow from within them" (John 7:37–38).

Jesus calls us to Himself because He wants to personally restore our joy by healing our bodies, minds, hearts, and spirits. He does this through the Rhythms of Delight we'll cover in this book: Worship, Word, Whisper, Wonder, and Walk. While these don't appear listed as such in Scripture, they're based on Jesus' own ways of relating to His Father, and I've found them essential in my own journey back to joy.

In His infinite wisdom and kindness, Jesus does not allow us to walk through darkness alone. God surrounded me with friends to speak wisdom and to work out these rhythms together—we

---

2. See Isaiah 61:1–5 and Luke 4:14–30.
3. See Luke 10:25–37. Jesus laid His hands on each sick person who came to Him, and He healed them (Luke 4:40). It's by His own wounds that Jesus offers us healing, until that glorious day when there will be no more sickness, sorrow, or death (see Isaiah 53:5 and Revelation 21:4).

prayed, cried, and worshiped together; we studied His Word and served one another; we went on nature walks with our kids together. Much of the work He's done in my life has come through the hands and feet of the people He's placed in my life. He led me to faith-based practitioners who taught me new ways of nourishing and moving my body to partner with His Spirit's work to restore my health. He also provided biblical counselors who helped me process the hard things and replace broken soundtracks with scriptural truths. And over time, Jesus restored my brokenness to delight.

While this second robber of delight might be invisible to many, the last one has become unfortunately common.

## Burnout

Some of us used to start the New Year with a fresh planner and ambitious goals—and even check off a lot of the boxes throughout the year—but excessive productivity and increasing responsibilities have led to continual busyness and eventual burnout. We dread facing our schedules bulging with commitments we'd rather avoid. We're burned-out on hyperactivity. We're burdened by nonstop caregiving for both elderly parents and younger children. And we feel a tiredness in our bones that no amount of sleep can erase.

A 2022 article from the American Psychological Association claims that symptoms of burnout and stress had increased 35 percent over the previous three years, citing physical fatigue, cognitive weariness, emotional exhaustion, or lack of interest, motivation, or energy.[4]

---

4. American Psychological Association, "Stress in America 2022: Concerned for the Future, Beset by Inflation," October 20, 2022, https://www.apa.org/news/press/releases/stress/2022/concerned-future-inflation.

Jesus knows what it's like to be stretched to capacity, and He saw it in His disciples too. Surrounded by people demanding their attention, Jesus and His disciples didn't even have time to eat. He said to them, "'*Come with me* by yourselves to a quiet place and and get some rest.' . . . So they went away by themselves in a boat to a solitary place" (Mark 6:31–32).

I find it humorous and slightly relatable that the only place the disciples could get away to be with Jesus was inside a boat in the middle of a lake. As a young mom, I experienced many days when the only place I could get a moment alone was in the bathroom, and even then, my children would stick their little fingers under the door to get my attention.

Jesus understands. And He meets us in our burnout with an invitation: "Come away with Me." In the second part of this book, we'll look at five Rhythms of Delight that can help us get away with Jesus even in the midst of the busyness and burnout of our lives.

If you're wondering if joy will ever come easily again—or worse, you won't ever feel delight again—I'm here to say joy can be yours. I know because I've experienced it myself, and I've seen joy resurface in friends and countless women I interact with around the country and in our online community.

No matter how the enemy comes at you to steal your joy, Jesus always meets you right where you are, with arms stretched wide and a heartfelt "Come to *Me*!" Only Jesus can deliver us from these robbers of delight. And thankfully Jesus longs to restore our joy: "Now is your time of grief, but I will see you again and you will rejoice, and no one will take away your joy" (John 16:22).[5]

Now take a few moments to consider: Where have you experienced burdens, brokenness, or burnout in your life? How long has this been going on? And how do you hear Jesus whispering to

5. See also Psalm 34:17–19.

your soul His invitation to "Come to Me" to restore you to healing and joy?

## The Darkest Day's Long Shadow

I've experienced all three robbers of delight over the years, but one theft in my early twenties struck like a fatal blow.

My father walked out on us one cold January night. I held open the screen door, staring out at him in shock, his face partially illuminated by the kitchen lights streaming through the doorway. He paused, suitcase in hand, only long enough to disown me and tell me not to contact him. Then he turned his back and walked away.

The breath whooshed out of my lungs like I'd been gut-punched. In the span of a few hours, I'd gone from feeling like a cherished daddy's girl to a discarded doll, and I hadn't seen it coming. I watched my father's car pull out of the driveway, the red tailgates fading into the darkness as he drove away.

The rest of that night and the weeks that followed remain a blur. I remember collapsing on the couch next to my sobbing mom. *How did we get here?* I wondered, hugging her close and trying to offer comfort while reeling from my father's parting words. I'd suspected their marriage was crumbling, but I'd never imagined he'd walk away from *me*. I never thought I'd become a disowned daughter.

Little did I know that this dark night would cast a gloom over the decade to come, overshadowing my joy in unsuspecting moments. *God, how could You let this happen? Where are You in this? Don't You care?* The accusations crept into my prayers over the following days, even while I struggled to quiet them.

I knew my father's actions were not God's fault, but I couldn't reconcile the goodness of a sovereign God with the brokenness of my family. So, I held on to hope that God would bring my father back to us.

## Breaking Down My Faith

Those first few months without my father remain mostly a blur. My new husband held me close as I grieved the loss of the larger-than-life man who had been both my dad and my pastor: the man who led me to Jesus in a Subaru one autumn night; the man who baptized me into the family of God; the man who taught me how to study my Bible inductively; the man who first trained me in public ministry.

He was gone, and his absence left a massive void in the heart of this grown-up daddy's girl.

My mom and I fervently prayed and fasted for his return. But weeks turned into months, which turned into years. And the yawning space left in his wake proved to be the testing ground of my faith.

*Is this really real?* I wondered, breaking apart the things I'd been taught about Jesus, examining them each piece by piece. *Is this really what I believe, even without my parents' faith to fall back on? And how do I rebuild my life when it feels like the foundation beneath my feet is crumbling?*

Ultimately, I didn't walk away—not because my faith was so strong, but because even in my wanderings, Jesus never left my side. He never let me forget the truth I bore in my very name: *God is my happiness.*

This isn't a story about recovering from parental estrangement. This is a story about Jesus' faithful love and tender presence even when your worst fears come true. It's a story about how God restores what the enemy has stolen, turning even evil into good.

# CHAPTER 2

# The God
# Who Delights

I've heard it said that we model our view of God after our earthly fathers. Perhaps you've heard this too. Maybe you've even noticed its truth in your own life.

If your father played with you in your childhood, you probably think God wants to spend time with you too.

If your father was short-tempered, you probably view God as easily angered too.

If your father shared your interests, you probably believe God is interested in you too.

If your father dropped everything to listen as you shared about your day, you're probably confident that God eagerly listens to you too.

If your father turned his back on you, literally or figuratively, you probably think God will turn His back on you too.

**As you reflect on your own relationship with your father, what memories come to mind that reinforce or confirm your thoughts about God? What other connections can you trace between the way you view your heavenly Father and your experience with your earthly one?**

Our fathers may have been all those things, all at the same time. This can make for a complicated childhood, requiring that we seek out godly counselors to process that cognitive dissonance. We can celebrate the good theology we've inherited from our parents while working to rewrite faulty views of God with scriptural portrayals of Him. For me, that meant reexamining my view of God as an angry Father.

## Sinners in the Hands of an Angry God?

You may have heard this quote from the influential American writer A. W. Tozer:

> What comes into our minds when we think about God is the most important thing about us. . . . We tend by a secret law of the soul to move toward our mental image of God. This is true not only of the individual Christian, but of the company of Christians that composes the Church. Always the most revealing thing about the Church is her idea of God.[1]

If Tozer is right, it's worth asking what mental image of God has shaped how we think and act. What vision of God compels us to share certain social media posts, to engage in heated debates in the comments, to rebuff (and even disown) brothers and sisters who vote differently than we do?

---

1. A. W. Tozer, *The Knowledge of the Holy* (New York: HarperCollins, 1978), 1.

The tone struck in many of these online arguments is one of anger and urgency, with some digital crusaders claiming that even Jesus overturned tables in the temple, so they're justified in lashing out at those deemed either too "woke" or too "conservative."

In some ways, the American church comes by her anger honestly. After all, one of the most influential sermons delivered on American soil is arguably Jonathan Edwards's 1741 message titled "Sinners in the Hands of an Angry God." (Ironically, attendees noted that Edwards delivered this harsh sermon in a calm tone, unlike many of today's internet-famous preachers.)

This vision of an angry God continued to color the American imagination for hundreds of years, and it's not uncommon to hear people referring to "the angry God of the Old Testament" juxtaposed with "the loving Jesus of the New Testament" (except, apparently, when He's overturning tables). But which view of God is really true? At His core, is He angry or kind? Short-tempered or long-suffering? Vengeful or compassionate?

Spend just a few minutes scrolling the comments section on any political-adjacent post on social media, and the presumed answer will become self-evident.

But is it possible we've subconsciously embraced a caricature of God that's not actually true? What if God is not, in fact, an angry deity stomping the heavenly courts, waiting to fling sinners into the fires of hell? What if He's not eager to dole out eternal punishments to those who deviate from traditional values? And what if there's really no difference between the Old Testament God and who He's revealed to be in the New Testament Jesus?

# The Most Important Thing About You

One thing I eagerly await in eternity is sitting down with great thinkers of the Christian faith and listening to their conversations. I wonder what they will agree on and where they'll push back. How fascinating those discussions will be.

So, imagine my delight when I discovered that the great C. S. Lewis responded to A. W. Tozer's now-famous one-liner in his book *The Weight of Glory*:

> I read in a periodical the other day that the fundamental thing is how we think of God. By God Himself, it is not! *How God thinks of us is not only more important, but infinitely more important.* . . . It is written that we shall "stand before" Him, shall appear, shall be inspected. The promise of glory is the promise, almost incredible and only possible by the work of Christ, that *some of us . . . shall please God.*
>
> To please God . . . *to be a real ingredient in the divine happiness* . . . to be loved by God, not merely pitied, but *delighted in as an artist delights in his work or a father in a son*—it seems impossible, a weight or burden of glory which our thoughts can hardly sustain. *But so it is.*[2]

Lewis most likely referred to a passage found in 2 Corinthians 5, where Paul describes how we will be united with God forever after our deaths, but in the meantime, His Spirit within us guides us to

---

2. C. S. Lewis, *The Weight of Glory* (New York: Macmillan Company, 1949), 10. Emphasis added. Whether Lewis inadvertently misquoted Tozer (leaving out the last words in the phrase "the most important thing about us") or whether Tozer himself changed his wording between the article's publication in 1941 and his book's publication in 1961 would be a fun journalistic investigation, but it just goes to show the importance of carefully choosing our words and also graciously assuming the best intentions about another.

please God while still in this mortal body: "We make it our aim to be pleasing to him" (v. 9).

We can easily jump to a moralistic interpretation—focusing our attention on how to behave, what to do, sins to avoid. But that completely misses the wonder of what's happening here. God cares about us so much that He's placed His Spirit in us, not primarily for behavior modification (though that will inevitably follow), but first and foremost for relationship, for connection, for ever-deepening delight.

I love how the seventeenth-century letters of Brother Lawrence describe this realty:

> The King, full of mercy and goodness, very far from chastising me, embraces me with love, makes me eat at His table, serves me with His own hands, gives me the key of His treasures; *He converses and delights Himself with me incessantly, in a thousand and a thousand ways, and treats me in all respects as His favourite.* It is thus I consider myself from time to time in His holy presence.[3]

That God cares about His pleasure in us and our pleasure in Him ought to stop us right now to raise a hallelujah. What an incredible thought! The God who created humankind doesn't begrudgingly put up with us as a disappointed parent tolerates a wayward child; He doesn't extend adoption to us out of distant pity. No, He welcomes us into relationship with Him as a Father who is greatly pleased with His children, charmed by their sincere efforts to please Him.

Even when our efforts to please God fall short, He joyfully covers the gaps. That's how much He delights in His children, in you and in me:

---

3. Brother Lawrence, *The Practice of the Presence of God* (Woodstock, Ontario: Devoted Publishing, 2018), 17. Emphasis added.

*To him who is able to keep you from stumbling and to present
you before his glorious presence without fault and with great
joy — to the only God our Savior be glory, majesty, power and
authority, through Jesus Christ our Lord, before all ages, now
and forevermore! Amen. (Jude 1:24–25)*

Did you catch that? God committed Himself to His people in such a way that He Himself will present us "without fault and with great joy." Linger with that truth for a moment. If you belong to the family of God, one day you'll hear His tender voice saying, "Well done. Enter into my eternal joy!"

> That God cares about His pleasure in us and our pleasure in Him ought to stop us right now to raise a hallelujah.

If this is true, and it is, we need to reclaim this view of a delightful God, to baptize our imaginations with the Scripture-rich claim that the dominant predisposition of our heavenly Father is not that of an angry God, but rather a joyful God, One who created us out of delight, redeems us for delight, and guides us into an eternal glory of delight.

Rather than allow our view of God to be shaped by imperfect parents or slanted sermons, we need to search the Scriptures for a true picture of His nature, His character, His person, and His joy. Let's see what the Bible has to say on this topic.

## The Heart of Our Creator Who Delights

We've seen how four influential men in the last three hundred years have portrayed God. But how does God describe Himself? How does He view us? What would He say is His own heart posture toward us? Is it one of anger or love? Vengeance or mercy? Tolerance or . . . delight?

These are not mere rhetorical questions. We need to counter-balance our earthly father's example by looking to Scripture for a true picture of God's nature, His character, His person, and His joy.

Trying to understand this theme of delight and joy in the Bible, I started with the first verse that came to mind: "*Take delight* in the LORD, and he will give you the desires of your heart" (Psalm 37:4). I looked up every verse that used the same Hebrew word translated "delight" above, and found that joy, happiness, delight, and desire are all interconnected in Psalm 34:5 (CSB), which famously states: "Those who look to him are radiant with joy; their faces will never be ashamed." And the Lord actually desires and delights in our well-being in Psalm 35:27: "May those who delight in my vindication shout for joy and gladness; may they always say, 'The Lord be exalted who delights in the well-being of his servant.'" Like an intricate web, each verse led to other passages that revealed how interconnected our joy and delight are to God's own pleasure in us.

Tracking down hundreds of references across each of the sixty-six books of the Bible, I found myself highlighting words like "joy," "delight," "celebration," and "rejoice" over and over again. I had no idea that the Bible had so much to say on the topic. I found that the Hebrew Scriptures use thirteen different words to capture the full meaning and variations of this idea of "delight," and that the Greek word for joy appears over two hundred times in the New Testament. Every word study, every cross reference, led me on the most delightful journey of going deeper into God's heart for His people.

The Hebrew word most often used to express delight in the Old Testament, *haphec*, means "a sense of joy and pleasure, experienced especially through achievements or relationships."[4] But

---

4. Word study on "*haphec*," J. Orr, gen. ed., *The International Standard Bible Encyclopedia*, 1915. As found in the Logos Bible study software program.

it's based on the root word that originally means "to bend," or "to incline to, take pleasure in," as used in Job 40:17 of the Behemoth's tail that "sways like a cedar." This may sound off-topic, but this picture of flexibility, of leaning toward something, can also represent an inclination of affection, a bending of one's heart and mind toward something—a magnetic attraction.

This idea of bending toward or leaning into? It's how God expresses His pleasure toward His people and in His people in Numbers 14:8, 2 Samuel 22:20, and Psalm 18:19, among many others.

It's how God describes His pleasure when people do right by another, as in Isaiah 66:4, Jeremiah 9:24, and Micah 7:18.

It describes humans' delight in God and His will in Psalm 40:8 and 73:25, but also their delight in others, like in Genesis 34:19, 1 Samuel 18:22, Esther 2:14, and Isaiah 66:3. God joyfully bends toward us, we joyfully bend toward God, and we joyfully bend toward each other.

Below I've included a sampling of verses that have become dear to me (many from the Christian Standard Bible). Pull out your pen and mark the words or phrases that resonate with you; I've italicized the parts that resonate with me.

## God Delights in His People

> For *the LORD takes pleasure in his people*;
> he adorns the humble with salvation. (Psalm 149:4 CSB)

> The LORD your God is among you,
> a warrior who saves.
> *He will rejoice over you with gladness.*
> He will be quiet in his love.
> *He will delight in you* with singing. (Zephaniah 3:17 CSB)

> *The LORD delights in those who fear him,*
> *who put their hope in his unfailing love.* (Psalm 147:11)

## God Delights in Our Salvation

> He brought me out to a spacious place;
> *he rescued me because he delighted in me.* (Psalm 18:19 CSB)[5]

> "But the one who boasts should boast in this:
> that he understands and knows me—
> that I am the LORD, *showing faithful love,*
> justice, and righteousness on the earth,
> for *I delight in these things.*
> This is the LORD's declaration." (Jeremiah 9:24 CSB)

> "I tell you, in the same way, there will be *more joy in heaven*
> over one sinner who repents than over ninety-nine righteous
> people who don't need repentance." (Luke 15:7 CSB)[6]

## God Delights in Jesus' Ministry

> "While he was still speaking, suddenly a bright cloud covered
> them, and a voice from the cloud said, 'This is *my beloved*
> *Son,* with whom *I am well-pleased.* Listen to him!'"
> (Matthew 17:5 CSB)

---

5. Consider too God's displeasure in the death of the wicked (Ezekiel 33:11 and 18:23) and how sincerely He desires the lost to turn to Him. God's heart longs for people to join in His pleasure by turning back to Him.
6. To my surprise, as I studied God's pleasure in His people, I started to see that His anger is born of love too, as in Hosea 14:4–5. Far from being a vengeful God bent on destroying "sinners," God's steadfast love compels us to return to Him and join in His pleasure. His long-suffering puts up with human folly for a long time, and His discipline toward His people always purposes to turn them back to Him.

"At that time he rejoiced in the Holy Spirit and said, 'I praise you, Father, Lord of heaven and earth, because you have hidden these things from the wise and intelligent and revealed them to infants. Yes, Father, because *this was your good pleasure.*'" (Luke 10:21 CSB)

"Now I am coming to you, and I speak these things in the world so that *they may have my joy completed in them.*" (John 17:13 CSB)

## God Delights in Our Future Together

"His master said to him, 'Well done, good and faithful servant! You were faithful over a few things; I will put you in charge of many things. *Share your master's joy.*'" (Matthew 25:23)

To him who is able to keep you from stumbling and to present you before his glorious presence without fault and *with great joy*—to the only God our Savior be glory, majesty, power and authority, through Jesus Christ our Lord, before all ages, now and forevermore! Amen. (Jude 1:24–25)

Then I heard a loud voice from the throne: Look, *God's dwelling is with humanity*, and he will live with them. They will be his peoples, and God himself will be with them and will be their God. (Revelation 21:3 CSB)

# Created for Love and Delight

Reading through these texts again simply takes my breath away. How expansive and intensive is God's delight in His own! Far from loving us out of obligation or duty, God loves us out of sheer delight, out of the overflow of the Trinity's joy in one another.

I've come to appreciate this definition of joy found in the book

*Joy Starts Here:* "Joy is the twinkle in someone's eyes, the smile from deep inside," and "the gladness that God feels when He makes His face shine over us, as in Numbers 6:24–26."[7]

When you understand that God's love and delight are intertwined in Scripture, you'll understand why Paul prayed for the early disciples and for us too:

> And I pray that you, being rooted and established in love, may have power, together with all the Lord's holy people, to grasp how wide and long and high and deep is the love of Christ, and to know this love that surpasses knowledge—that you may be filled to the measure of all the fullness of God. (Ephesians 3:17–19)

Empowered by God's divine strength, we begin to comprehend a fraction of the immeasurable love our perfect Father extends toward us. His heart bends and beats with delight . . . for us.

Regardless of your earthly father's impact, I hope you feel that deep, affirming murmur of love coming from your heavenly Father.

And I hope this unified overview of God's utter delight in His people from Genesis to Revelation allays our unease that "the Old Testament God" is wrathful while "the New Testament God" is loving. Our God is the same, yesterday, today, and forever.

But if we're still holding on to vestiges of doubt, let's take a closer look at the life of Jesus, and how He reveals the Father's heart of delightful love toward His people.

## God Wants to Restore Your Joy

Joy and delight are at the heart of God's good plan for His people. From the first pronouncement of "very good" when He

---

7. E. James Wilder et al., *Joy Starts Here: The Transformation Zone* (East Peoria, IL: Shepherd's House, Inc., 2013), 237.

stepped back to admire the creation He'd just completed, to the promise of coming to dwell with us again in the last chapter of the Bible, the thrust of the gospel is this invitation to a relationship of mutual delight.

Every beautiful gift that has ever brought a smile to your face held within it a kernel of God's affection for you. Every baby's laugh, every painted sunset, every comfortable hug expresses your heavenly Father's pleasure in you. For every good and perfect gift comes from God above.

And because God already delights in His children, we can learn to delight again, to recapture the childlike wonder of a life lived with Him. You will learn to delight in the Lord because you have a God who already delights in you. And the next chapter will begin to show us the way.

# CHAPTER 3

# God Cares About Your Joy

"God cares about your holiness, not your happiness," the preacher announced at the youth rally. I dutifully took notes, writing the words in my journal, wondering all the while if they were true. I heard this refrain many times throughout my adolescence, being told that following Jesus was a call to somber self-denial, eschewing earthly pleasure for the sake of a future reward in heaven. Anything that was too much fun was suspect, from playing dress-up to playing soccer on Sundays.

And while the soul-forming process of following Jesus involves growing pains, pitting holiness against happiness is a false dichotomy that's misdirected at best and harmful at worst. God actually cares about our happiness, even more than we do.

That's a bold claim, but before we delve into a study of this theme in Scripture, you may be wondering if there's a difference between joy and happiness. In short, there's not. The Hebrew and Greek words for *joy* and *happy* are used interchangeably throughout Scripture and carry with them connotations of delight, pleasure, and fulfillment. Pastor and theologian John Piper explains:

If you have nice little categories for "joy is what Christians have" and "happiness is what the world has," you can scrap those when you go to the Bible, because the Bible is indiscriminate in its uses of the language of happiness and joy and contentment and satisfaction.[1]

In other words, God is the inventor of both joy and happiness, and He lavishes both on His creation, like a partying child tosses confetti.[2]

As one C. S. Lewis scholar summarizes: "God is Love, and Love is at the center of the universe. He created human beings, in His image, in order that they might participate in this joyful communion of love."[3] And lest we think that this emphasis on being created for delight is some progressive notion, consider that when God formed Adam and Eve, He placed them not in a wilderness but in a luscious garden filled with breathtaking beauty, luxurious provision, and His own personal presence. We know this garden was called Eden, but did you know that the Hebrew word Eden literally means "the place of delight"? Sit with that for a moment. Our Maker formed humanity and created our first home to be a garden of delight. His heart for us has always overflowed with love and pleasure.[4]

---

1. John Piper, "Let Your Passion Be Single," Desiring God, November 12, 1999, https://www.desiringgod.org/messages/let-your-passion-be-single.
2. On God's indiscriminate lavishing of happiness on all, see Matthew 5:45.
3. Connie Hintz (2008), "The Theme of Desire in the Writings of C. S. Lewis: Implications for Spiritual Formation," Inklings Forever: Published Colloquium Proceedings 1997–2016: Vol. 6, Article 8.
4. The Klein Dictionary, a scholarly etymological dictionary of rabbinic Hebrew, explains that Eden comes from a Hebrew root word that means "pleasure, delight, luxury." It was the rabbinic way of trying to capture the wonder and utter delights of humans' first home. Sefaria. Klein Dictionary, עֵדֶן.1. Carta Jerusalem, 1st edition, 1987. https://www.sefaria.org/Klein_Dictionary.

Sin entered the garden of Eden (and indeed enters our own lives) when we humans tried to fabricate happiness for ourselves apart from communion with God, the divine source of all pleasure, comfort, and joy.

Lewis famously quips:

> It would seem that our Lord finds our desires, not too strong, but too weak. We are half-hearted creatures, fooling about with drink and sex and ambition when infinite joy is offered us, like an ignorant child who wants to go on making mud pies in a slum because he cannot imagine what is meant by the offer of a holiday at the sea. We are far too easily pleased.[5]

It's not our desire for happiness that God disapproves of; it's our attempts to satisfy that desire outside of Him. As much as we might long for our lives to be characterized by joy, happiness, and delight, God wants this for us even more.

After all, it's God's own desire and delight to set apart for Himself a people of His very own, that we would declare His excellencies for all eternity (see 1 Peter 2:9). In other words, our holiness is the overflow of God's happiness, which leads to our own happiness. Because Jesus is the eternal source of our lasting joy, learning to delight in Jesus is the shift that brings meaning and enjoyment to all our other pursuits this side of heaven.

**Our holiness is the overflow of God's happiness, which leads to our own happiness.**

God knows that we will only find true joy and fulfillment in Him alone, so He placed within our hearts a deep desire that will keep driving us to Himself. Augustine wrote of this very force hundreds

---

5. C. S. Lewis, *The Weight of Glory*, 2.

of years ago: "Thou movest us to delight in praising Thee; for Thou hast formed us for Thyself, and our hearts are restless till they find rest in Thee."[6] In this sense, even the desire for joy comes from God Himself, as a means of drawing us to Himself.

Our holiness is not antithetical to our happiness, but rather part of becoming truly happy in God Himself. A happy soul is a Christlike soul, and a Christlike soul is a happy soul. The writer of Psalm 119 expresses this dynamic: "In the way of your testimonies I delight as much as in all riches. . . . Lead me in the path of your commandments, for I delight in it. . . . My soul keeps your testimonies; I love them exceedingly" (vv. 14, 35, 167 ESV).

How much more we, who get to see the fulfillment of those commands in the life, death, and resurrection of Jesus, can marvel at their wonder and rejoice in their fulfillment.

## Blessed Are the Happy

But does Jesus actually talk about our joy?

He does, though we miss it in our English translations of the Bible. In the Sermon on the Mount, when teaching what life in His kingdom looks like, Jesus begins by describing *happiness*. I didn't see this until recently, when studying the Sermon on the Mount and looking up the word our Bibles translate "blessed." If you're unfamiliar with the Beatitudes or simply need a refresher, they start like this:

> "Blessed are the poor in spirit,
>     for theirs is the kingdom of heaven.
> Blessed are those who mourn,
>     for they will be comforted.

6. Augustine, *The Confessions: With an Introduction and Contemporary Criticism* (San Francisco: Ignatius Press, 2012), 1.1.5.

Blessed are the meek,
    for they will inherit the earth." (Matthew 5:3–5)

When Jesus describes life in His kingdom, He starts not with a command for holiness but an upside-down description of happiness. The word that's translated as "blessed" is actually a Greek translation of the Hebrew word *ashrei*, better rendered "oh how fortunate," "oh how happy," "oh how flourishing," or "oh how blessed." As one scholar explains, *ashrei* "is a particle interjection that means 'how happy' (from the root that means to walk righteously in joy) that is often used in the Psalms."[7]

In other words, when Jesus is given the opportunity to explain life in the kingdom of God, He begins with an explanation of what it means to be truly happy. And unlike the way most of us read the Beatitudes, "The blessing/baruch is in the second line, not the first line. The perspective's in the first line, *ashrei*, and it's a super-twist, and the blessing is in the second line."[8]

God's blessing is that He offers His kingdom: He gives it to those who are powerless, and those who receive it are truly happy.

God's blessing is His comfort: He gives it to those who mourn, and they who receive it are truly happy.

God's blessing is giving earth as an inheritance: He gives it to those who are humble, and those who receive it are truly happy.

7. "The Beatitudes," Hebrew for Christians, accessed March 15, 2024, https://www.hebrew4christians.com/Scripture/Brit_Chadashah/Beatitudes/beatitudes.html#loaded.
8. "What Does 'Blessed' Mean? (Beatitudes, Pt. 1)," BibleProject, January 22, 2024, https://bibleproject.com/podcast/what-does-blessed-mean-beatitudes-pt-1/.

Reading through the Beatitudes in this manner reveals that God cares tremendously about our happiness and knows that true happiness is found when we turn to Him to fulfill all our needs and desires.

## Joy That Is Complete

Not only did Jesus start His teaching ministry with this theme of true happiness, He ended with it too.

The night before He was betrayed, on the hardest night of His life, He spoke to His disciples about joy: "I have told you these things so that my joy may be in you and your joy may be complete" (John 15:11). Jesus is actually preoccupied with our joy because He wants us to avail ourselves of the pleasure and happiness found only in Him. Jonathan Edwards, the same person who preached "Sinners in the Hands of an Angry God," wasn't all fire and brimstone. He explains: "The happiness Christ gives to his people is a participation of his own happiness."[9]

While indeed the call to follow Jesus is a call to die to ourselves and pick up our crosses, it's ultimately a call to follow Him. It is a call to ultimate happiness because it's an invitation to "participate in this joyful communion of love," as Lewis reminded us. To walk as Jesus walked. To live as He lives. To love as He loves. I use the present tense here because His ministry on earth has not ended. He continues to lovingly guide and shepherd us from His place at the Father's right hand through His Spirit's indwelling presence in us.

This call to follow Jesus is rooted in love: God's love for His Son, the Son's love for us, and our love-response toward Him and

---

9. Owen Strachan and Douglas Allen Sweeney, *The Essential Jonathan Edwards: An Introduction to the Life and Teaching of America's Greatest Theologian* (Chicago: Moody Publishers, 2018), Kindle.

one another. Love, joy, and delight are scripturally inseparable, not just in Jesus' last words to His disciples but throughout Scripture and throughout Jesus' own life.

## Joy at the Heart of the Gospel

If this theme of joy and delight is whispered in the Old Testament, it shouts in the gospel accounts of Jesus' life and ministry. Read through any account of Jesus' life, and you'll see how He makes visible the Father's heart of delight throughout His earthly ministry and beyond:

### Joy at Jesus' birth

When the angel announced Jesus' birth to the shepherds, he called it "good news of great joy that will be for all the people" (Luke 2:10 ESV). The Greek here actually means "mega." Mega-joy. Enormous joy. Joy multiplied with more joy. And this joy is available not just for the religious elite or a certain ethnic group, but for all people, including you and me. Mega-joy awaits us, friend.

### Joy in the simple pleasures of life

Jesus regularly hung out with friends at meals, so much so that it became a sticking point for the Pharisees, who accused Him of being "a glutton and a drunkard." Of course, He was neither, but the fact that He enjoyed God's good, earthly gifts redeems the goodness of being a fully embodied human. Jesus' actions stood in direct defiance of the platonic dualistic claim that the spiritual is more pure than physical.

### Joy in inviting all into friendship

Jesus regularly created room at the table for all people to come to Him and was accused of being "a friend of tax collectors and sinners" (Matthew 11:19), regularly enjoying fun meals that irked the buttoned-up legalists (see 9:11–17). This was a time to rejoice because the kingdom of heaven had finally come!

### Joy in children

Imagine Jesus' delight in welcoming the little children to come to Him. While the text doesn't explicitly mention joy here, anyone who's spent any time around little kids giggling and having a good time can't keep a grumpy face for long. Unless you feel like they're interrupting your plans, which is exactly the reaction Jesus rebukes in His disciples. Imagine the utter delight on Jesus' face as He opens His arms wide to bring those kiddos into a group hug.

The disciples were scandalized by the inconvenience, but Jesus was certainly enjoying Himself and the kids who had come to Him. Hear the delight in His voice as He certainly spoke the Aaronic blessing over the children: "The LORD bless you and keep you; the LORD make his face shine upon you and be gracious toward you; the LORD turn his face toward you and give you peace" (Numbers 6:24–26). Here is joy. Here is God's delight in the welfare of His children (see Psalm 35:27).

### Joy when the lost come home

In His parables about the lost sheep, the lost coin, and the lost son, Jesus offers illustrations to help us understand the joy of salvation. Surprisingly, this joy reverberates not only in the one who is rescued, but also in the Father's heart: "There will be more rejoicing in heaven over one sinner who repents . . . there is rejoic-

ing in the presence of the angels of God over one sinner who repents . . . we had to celebrate and be glad, because this brother of
yours was dead and is alive again; he was lost and is found" (Luke
15:5–7, 9–10, 31–32). God Himself is overcome with joy when
someone responds "yes" to His invitation, and that's how He feels
about you and me too.

*Joy in working through us and revealing new things to us*

When Jesus' disciples return with a report of all the great things
they did in His name (even causing demons to scramble), Jesus
responds with great rejoicing and thanks the Father for revealing spiritual truths to His own because it was His "good pleasure"
(Luke 10:17–24). Notice that all three members of the Trinity
are rejoicing here: God's Holy Spirit is filling and moving Jesus
to rejoice with great joy in the Father's pleasure; that is, revealing
the hidden things to His children—that's us. God takes great joy
in revealing Himself to us in new and deeper ways, helping us delight in Him more and more.

*Joy motivated Jesus' ultimate sacrifice*

Even in His most agonizing moments on the cross, it was love
expressed as joy that kept Jesus there: "For the joy that lay before
him, he endured the cross, despising the shame, and sat down at
the right hand of the throne of God" (Hebrews 12:2 CSB).

*Joy at Jesus' resurrection*

The darkness of Jesus' betrayal, beating, and death finds brilliant counterbalance in His glorious resurrection. Death itself
was swallowed up in victory as Jesus emerged victorious from the
grave! Imagine Mary's joy upon hearing her name in that tender

voice she thought she'd never hear again. Imagine Jesus' delight in reuniting with His friends again in the upper room, sitting down for a meal together again. Imagine His sheer joy in explaining how the Scriptures were all coming true while He strolled with the disciples toward Emmaus, while "their hearts burned within them" with strong emotions, then bursting with joy as they ran to tell the others what they'd just experienced (see Luke 24:13–35). Joy is stamped all over Jesus' marvelous resurrection.

### Joy at the gift of the Holy Spirit

Jesus told His disciples that it was better for them that He go to the Father because they would receive the incredible, empowering, priceless gift of His own Spirit residing within them. And when God's Spirit came down upon them, they celebrated with so much joy and delight that onlookers thought them drunk. The Spirit of God not only produces joy in the hearts of believers but is uniquely connected to joy throughout the New Testament.[10]

### Joy at Jesus' return for His bride

Again and again, Jesus describes the future fulfillment of His promises as a party, a wedding, a celebration of epic proportions. After all, what do wedding festivities look like? They're fun, enjoyable, loud . . . and for the bride and groom finally united in marriage, it's an experience of sheer delight.

Oh, friend, I hope these pages are all marked up in your book, for this is the heart of Jesus for you and for me. Joy radiates off the pages of the Gospels because Jesus is the embodiment of the Father's delight in His own. What we see in Jesus, we can know to be true about the Father, because Jesus is "the image of the in-

---

10. See Luke 10:21, 1 Thessalonians 1:6–7, and Romans 14:17.

visible God" (Colossians 1:15). And while no one has ever seen God, the Word made flesh in Jesus "has revealed him" (John 1:18 csb), and what we see poured out on the pages of the Gospels is love and delight, joy and rejoicing.

Author Dane Ortlund explains it this way: "Here is the promise of the gospel and the message of the whole Bible: In Jesus Christ, we are given a friend who will always enjoy rather than refuse our presence."[11] The whole of the gospel message is not merely that we are justified in Jesus and have a future in heaven, but also that because of this justification, we are invited deeper into the presence of God to enjoy friendship with Him forever—starting here and now, right where we are.

Jesus Himself explains, on that last night with His disciples, "No longer do I call you servants, for the servant does not know what his master is doing; but I have called you friends, for all that I have heard from my Father I have made known to you" (John 15:15 esv).

Whoa. Can this really be true for us too or was Jesus just talking about His twelve closest disciples?

## An Invitation into Joyful Friendship

In Revelation 3:20, the risen Jesus says to Christians in the early church: "Behold, I stand at the door and knock. If anyone hears my voice and opens the door—" **How would you finish that sentence? What do you imagine Jesus may want to do with you?** "I will come in to him and eat with him, and he with me" (esv). Jesus wants to spend time with you. He wants to linger over a meal together. To listen to you share about your day. To offer His insights

---

11. Dane Ortlund, *Gentle and Lowly: The Heart of Christ for Sinners and Sufferers* (Wheaton, IL: Crossway, 2020), 114.

into your struggles. To deepen your acquaintance with each other, day after day after blessed day.

Don't miss this: if you belong to Jesus, He is indeed your Savior, but He also wants to be your closest friend.

A true friend enjoys spending time with you. A true friend draws near to you. A true friend shares their most tender thoughts and hopes with you. Is this too much to hope for in our relationship with Jesus? It is not.

Consider the words of Richard Sibbes, an Anglican theologian and contemporary of Shakespeare (and whose language may remind you of high school literature class). He speaks of friendship with Jesus like this:

> In friendship there is a mutual consent, a union of judgment and affections. There is a mutual sympathy in the good and ill of another . . .
>
> In friendship, there is mutual solace and comfort one in another. *Christ delights himself in his love to the church, and his church delights herself in her love to Christ.*[12]

Mutual delight. As Jesus delights in His bride, so we are invited to delight in Him. And this delight leads to true happiness and joy as we experience the blessings of friendship with God.

This is the heart of the triune God for us: Father, Son, and Holy Spirit, all delighting in those they created for delight.

But if this is true, why do so many of us lack this delightful friendship with God in our day-to-day lives? And why do so many

---

12. Richard Sibbes, *Bowels Opened*, 2:37, as quoted in Dane Ortlund's *Gentle and Lowly*, 119. Emphasis added. I'm deeply indebted to Ortlund's book on the heart of Jesus for bringing Sibbes' work to my attention, and for refreshing my perspective on what friendship with Jesus can look like for Christians today.

of us experience the Christian life as a call to deprivation rather than delight?

Perhaps it's because we've exchanged the call to friendship with a focus on rules and restrictions.

## The Problem with Joyless Spiritual Disciplines

Many of us make New Years' resolutions to read our Bibles or pray more. I get emails weekly from readers around the world who share their genuine desire to be more disciplined but lack consistency. Many Christians want to "do quiet time" because it's the "right thing to do." But what if this is the wrong focus? A checklist mentality has us read a certain number of Bible chapters on a strict schedule; we do it, believing that more information will lead to heart transformation, but this kind of quiet time can leave us bored, overwhelmed, or guilty when we fall behind on these "disciplines." No wonder there's no joy.

**When it comes to our spiritual formation, we don't have a discipline problem; we have a delight problem.**

God wired our brains to seek out pleasurable activities. It's no hardship to eat dessert, watch a fun show, or sit by a crackling fire. Those activities are easy precisely because they're enjoyable. We don't need discipline to do what delights us.

So, when it comes to our spiritual formation, we don't have a discipline problem; we have a delight problem. If we're simply "doing quiet time" because it's good for us, we're missing the point.

The problem with joyless spiritual disciplines is that we're missing Jesus in them. When we separate the practice from the Person, we miss the power of His presence. And all along, Jesus is patiently standing at the door, knocking, waiting.

What if we shifted our focus from "doing quiet time" to deepening our friendship with Jesus? Here's what that could look like:

- Instead of reading a few chapters to "keep up" with our reading plan, we search the Scriptures to get to know the heart of Jesus (see John 5:39–47).

- Instead of mumbling religious jargon before meals, we have a conversational chat with Jesus before we eat, check back in after we eat, and keep the conversational flow going all day (see 1 Thessalonians 5:17).

- Instead of venting our frustrations about today's politics or gossiping about a high profile person's latest post, we go for a walk around the neighborhood and talk to Jesus about it, listening to how He responds (see Isaiah 9:6, where Jesus is called "Wonderful Counselor").

What if our spiritual disciplines were never meant to be isolated religious activities but rather rhythms of deepening friendship with Jesus?

## Channels of Adoration

When we truly understand God's invitation to mutual delight through friendship in Jesus, every aspect of life becomes an opportunity to experience Him. It's not just the exercise of spiritual disciplines that offers a vehicle into God's happiness, but the entirety of our earthly experience. With God, there is no secular-sacred divide, for all of earth is filled with His glory, and every good gift can become a channel of adoration.

In *Letters to Malcolm*, C. S. Lewis writes:

> I have tried, since that moment, to *make every pleasure into a channel of adoration.* I don't mean simply by giving thanks for it. One must of course give thanks, but I mean something different. . . .
>
> This sweet air whispers of the country from whence it blows. It is a message. *We know we are being touched by a finger of that right hand at which there are pleasures for evermore.* There need be no question of thanks or praise as a separate event, something done afterwards. To experience the tiny theophany is itself to adore.
>
> Gratitude exclaims, very properly: "How good of God to give me this." Adoration says: "What must be the quality of that Being whose far-off and momentary coruscations are like this!" *One's mind runs back up the sunbeam to the sun.*[13]

When I see a beautiful sunset, I can both enjoy its beauty and, in my enjoyment, adore the One who by His creativity painted the horizon with such beauty. "How good of God to give me this."

When I hold a baby in my arms and breathe in their newborn scent, I can both enjoy this infant and, in my enjoyment, marvel at the Creator who made them in His own image.

When I linger over a good meal with good friends, I can both enjoy their companionship and, in my enjoyment, delight in the One whose love offers us friendship as an echo of His own.

This "earthy" spirituality brings the whole range of human experience into an awareness of God's presence with us, His delight

---

13. C. S. Lewis, *Letters to Malcolm: Chiefly on Prayer* (New York: Harcourt, 1992), 88–90, https://www.cslewisinstitute.org/resources/reflections-why-not-begin-with-this/. Emphasis added.

in us, and His invitation to delight in Him. All of life—not just our morning devotions—is an opportunity to enjoy God.

We can't separate our spiritual growth activities from our hobbies, leisure, or fun pursuits because God is equally present through His Spirit in all of it. And because Jesus is the eternal source of our lasting joy, learning to delight in Him will sanctify our enjoyment of other pursuits this side of heaven. As James attests: "Every good and perfect gift is from above, coming down from the Father of the heavenly lights, who does not change like shifting shadows" (James 1:17).

The rest of this book will challenge us to reimagine the daily rhythms of our lives lived with Jesus. This invitation to a life of delight and eternal joy may seem too good to be true, especially if you feel like you're too busy, broken, or burdened to really experience this promise.

But in our place of darkest despair, Jesus is already standing close, arms outstretched to embrace us.

## Jesus, Don't You Care?

On this journey of learning to delight again in Jesus, I experienced the sudden onset of the darkest storm of my life. Tossed by fierce waves of health crises, relational challenges, new responsibilities, mental anguish, and spiritual warfare, I felt like each hour brought a new setback, sapping more of my resilience and ability to stay afloat. *Why am I going through all this?* I wondered. *God, where are You in this storm?*

Tears were my constant companions day and night, and I struggled to get out of bed in the morning for fear of what else might happen over the course of that day. I'd experienced God's faithfulness over the years, so although I didn't doubt His goodness, I didn't sense His presence. And that troubled me.

I reached out with my prayers but felt only darkness. *Why can't I seem to grab hold of You, God?*

Silence.

And chaos.

And gradually . . . fear.

I reached out to friends and family to ask them to pray. I scheduled an appointment with my godly counselor. I took extra time to sleep, to eat nutritious foods, and to get outside. But none of it seemed to help. I began wondering what Jesus was doing. Did He hear? Did He see? *Did He care?* Like Peter sinking under the waters, I felt like one more wave would send me under. And like the disciples caught in the fierce storm, I felt like Jesus was napping in the stern.

At one point, my husband found me at the kitchen sink, tears rolling down my cheeks. He walked toward me with open arms, and I stepped into his embrace. "I've given everything I have, and it's still not enough," I sobbed onto his shoulder. He held me close, rubbing my back, while whispering in my ear assurances that no, I was not crazy, and no, I was not a burden, and no, God's not finished with me yet.

My dear husband held on and wouldn't let me go, even after the tears subsided. He held me tight, and eventually, I leaned my weight into his frame, letting his strong arms support me. I didn't have to hold myself together anymore because my sweet husband was holding me. *This is how Jesus holds us*, I thought.

"Hold me, Jesus," I whispered in my heart. "Please be my strength because I don't have any more." Those words rolled over each other, again and again, the only prayers I could manage in the deafening celestial silence.

## Leaning into Jesus' Embrace

In my journal, I wrote out my confusion and despair: "Why can't I see Your goodness here? Why do I feel all alone? Why can't I seem to pull myself out of this funk? What is wrong with me? Why are tears just below the surface? And where are You? What are You doing here? Don't You care?"[14] The tone was not demanding, but desperate.

As I was writing, a verse came to mind, as if in response to those questions: "The Lord is faithful, and he will strengthen you and protect you from the evil one" (2 Thessalonians 3:3).

Faithful. Jesus is *faithful*: He keeps His promises; He is trustworthy; He is consistent to His character.

In the midst of sorrow, heartache, and darkness, even though I wasn't feeling Him, Jesus was strengthening me and protecting me from the evil one. And just as He prayed for Peter (Luke 22:32), so He prays for us: that our faith would not fail, that His strength would make us endure the evil one, that we may strengthen others with His strength in us and comfort others with the comfort we ourselves receive.

Though we falter, we do not fall because Jesus holds us fast. Even when we may not see what Jesus is doing *through* these hardships, we can trust what He is doing *in* them: praying for us, strengthening us, protecting us, *holding us*.

We can lean into Him in times of trouble. Rather than driving us away from our Savior, we can choose to bend toward Him as the winds and the storm batter us.

Lean in. Bend close. Stay by His side.

---

14. This last question echoes Jesus' own disciples' despair at the threat of drowning in a storm, while He was napping in the stern. See Mark 4:35–41.

## Suffering with Jesus

It may seem odd to discuss suffering in a book devoted to the topic of delight and joy, but pain is an unavoidable part of life. If we're to develop a biblical understanding of what it means to delight in Jesus, we must account for those seasons of life where we're pummeled by suffering, grief, and sorrow. Jesus comforted His disciples with the assurance that "in this world you will have trouble. But take heart! I have overcome the world" (John 16:33).

It's not the absence of suffering that makes for a joy-filled life; it's Jesus' presence with us in the hardship, leading us ever deeper with Him. He, the Man of Sorrows, knows what it's like to endure physical torment, emotional trauma, and spiritual agony. He knows what it's like to be tempted and taunted by the enemy of our souls. He knows what it's like for your body to feel frail, broken, and dying.

If we want to know Jesus, to truly walk with Him in close friendship, then we must learn to lean into Him in both our joys and sorrows. As Paul wrote, "I want to know Christ—yes, to know the power of his resurrection *and* participation in his sufferings" (Philippians 3:10). We cannot experience one without the other.

And because He knows what it's like to be truly human, Jesus welcomes us to come to Him to find help in our time of need.[15] He is with us through the darkest valley and in the deepest abyss.[16] When we don't know what to pray, His own Spirit groans with us and for us.[17] And His grip on us is so secure, nothing can snatch us out of His hand or separate us from His presence.[18]

---

15. See Hebrews 4:16.
16. See Psalms 23:4 and 139:7–12.
17. See Romans 8:26–27 and Hebrews 7:25.
18. See John 10:28 and Romans 8:35–39.

This is why it's possible for us to rejoice even in our suffering, not because we're masochists who enjoy the pain, but because in the pain we experience the closeness and comfort of Jesus' presence in a special way.[19] As Elisabeth Elliot discovered, we can be confident that suffering is never for nothing, for:

> The deepest things that I have learned in my own life have come from the deepest suffering. And out of the deepest waters and the hottest fires have come the deepest things that I know about God. And I imagine that most of you would say exactly the same.[20]

We fix our eyes on Jesus, even as we walk through suffering, because He knows what it's like to suffer, and it's from His presence that we draw strength:

> For the joy set before him he endured the cross, scorning its shame, and sat down at the right hand of the throne of God. Consider him who endured such opposition from sinners, so that you will not grow weary and lose heart. (Hebrews 12:2–3)

It's in our place of suffering that we discover this unique aspect of what it means to delight in the Lord—not jumping with exuberant joy, but quietly leaning into His embrace.

## When Delight Isn't Joyful

The quiet assurance of Jesus' steadfast presence got me through that season of torrential blows. I couldn't see Him. I didn't feel

---

19. See Romans 5:3–5 and James 1:2–4.
20. Elisabeth Elliot, *Suffering Is Never for Nothing* (Nashville: B&H Publishing Group, 2019). Kindle, 30.

Him. But I knew, to the marrow of my bones, that Jesus wasn't standing idly by.

Jesus was holding me.

Jesus was strengthening me.

Jesus was interceding for me.

And as I shifted my attention from "Where are You?" to "What are You doing right now?" I felt a quiet reassurance that I didn't have to hold on so tight—because He was holding me.

I was still weepy. I was still exhausted. I was still spent, but I was safe—because Jesus was holding me, and He would not let go.

Through those troubling weeks of torment, I learned that delight isn't always joyful.

Remember the original meaning of the Hebrew word most often translated "delight" in the Old Testament? It's "to bend toward" or "to lean into."[21]

This "delight" is like a good friend who perches on the edge of her seat, listening with rapt attention to not miss a single detail. It's like a husband who gathers his wife in his arms, holding her tight and rubbing her back, whispering in her ear, "I've got you," every time she sobs, "I don't have anything left to give."

"I've got you."

Bending close, leaning in, holding tight. Delight. Not joyful, but still present, still choosing to remain, to abide, to stay close, to bend down. Because he delights in her.

I wonder if that's a picture of how Jesus delights in us, even in our sorrow—leaning in, holding tight, His strong arms pulsing love and strength into our frail bodies when we have nothing left to give.

---

21. James Strong, *A Concise Dictionary of the Words in the Greek Testament and The Hebrew Bible* (Bellingham, WA: Logos Bible Software, 2009), 7.

He's got you.

That's how I learned the depth of Jesus' delight in that season, even when there was no joy. *Especially because there was no joy.* His grip never faltered, and His delight never wavered. He bent down low to listen to my cries for help, and He held me close when I had no strength left to hold on to Him. And yes, Jesus used my husband's literal arms to paint a picture of His delight in me.

If you're in a season of sorrow and despair, know that you're not alone: Jesus holds you securely. You can rest in Him. Lean into friends and family who can support you and feed you and care for you when you're most vulnerable. Seek medical attention if you need that. Jesus works through all kinds of people to care for us and keep us safe.

Regardless of your season, look around and ask: "What are You doing, Jesus?" Scripturally, we have many of the answers:

- He is holding us

- He is praying for us

- He is purifying us

- He is protecting us

- He is strengthening us

Search the Scriptures and find more of Jesus' ongoing work on your behalf, even now, from His place at the Father's right hand.

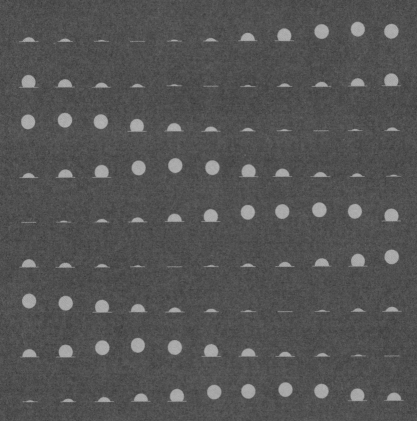

PART TWO

# Rhythms to Restore Joy

# CHAPTER 4

# Restoring Your Brain's Pathway to Joy

Expand my capacity for joy," I whispered in prayer, right hand resting on my forehead, right there in the middle of the coffee shop.

For months following that conversation with Carol at the conference, I'd been studying this topic of joy in the Bible and in science. I checked out all the books on the topic that I could get my hands on, at one point maxing out my library card—at two different library systems. Yep. I had books stacked in my living room, next to my bed, in my car, and in my purse. I was reading on this topic every spare moment. When I want to learn something new, I dive in deep.

What I learned about joy crosses many fields of discipline, not just biblical studies but also brain science, psychology, metabolic health, relational attachments, exercise science, sleep health, and more. Every scientific discovery affirms how wonderfully our

Creator knit us together—mind, body, heart, and spirit—and I learned that we cannot ignore one aspect of our selves while seeking wholeness in the others. So, I started asking God to heal every part of me. I believe that God will someday grant us glorified bodies and fully sanctified minds, hearts, and spirits; but we can ask our Maker to begin a work of healing and restoration even now.

What follows in this chapter and the rest of this book comes not only from this extensive research, but also from what I discovered on my own personal journey with Jesus. He has, indeed, restored my joy, but I learned it's not a once-and-done transaction—instead, every day, He is increasing my capacity to receive and experience His joy.

I've done my very best to cite sources and make interdisciplinary connections wherever I could, but I also endeavored to keep things simple and clear. Every page that follows has been prayed over, rewritten, edited, and reviewed for accuracy.[1] But every year we learn and discover new things, so please read this book in community, discuss what you're learning with others, and practice new rhythms together.

A word to fellow habit junkies: the whole industry that has sprung up around productivity and self-improvement would have us believe we're machines that require just a few basic tweaks to operate at optimal effectiveness.

*We are not machines.* We are humans created in the image of God, and our patterns of living inevitably change from one season to the next, whether we're welcoming a new baby into the family, moving to a new state, shifting from the school year into

---

1. I'm deeply indebted to *Atomic Habits* by James Clear and *Tiny Habits* by Stanford Professor BJ Fogg for introducing me to many of the concepts included in this chapter. I've also found helpful Justin Whitmel Earley's book *The Common Rule: Habits of Purpose in an Age of Distraction.*

summer break, becoming an aging parent's primary caregiver, nursing an injury, or a myriad of life changes. We are more like a garden than a gadget—we grow slowly with patient nurturing and care through many seasons, even when it seems like nothing (or everything) is changing.[2]

That's why I've chosen to use the term "rhythms" to describe this process. As we'll see, joy is always relational, and growth is always seasonal, so consider Scripture's invitation to a flourishing life with God, for the one who delights in Him:

> That person is like a tree planted by streams of water,
>     which yields its fruit in season
> and whose leaf does not wither—
>     whatever they do prospers. (Psalm 1:3)

I want to be that tree, the one that drinks up refreshing water from the nearby stream, the one whose roots go deep, the one that bears luscious fruit in the right season, the one whose leaf does not wither because it's nourished by the rich soil: "Remain in me, as I also remain in you. No branch can bear fruit by itself; it must remain in the vine" (John 15:4).

## Why One-Size-Fits-All Formulas Never Work

While we'll discuss lots of different rhythms grounded in Scripture and science, what you won't find here is a formula. That's

---

2. In recent years I've been pleased to find more books addressing this hyper-productivity focus in our generation and helping us reframe our understanding of what it means to be human in refreshingly honest reflections. If you'd like to read more about this, I recommend Jennifer Dukes Lee's *Growing Slow*, Mary Marantz's *Slow Growth Equals Strong Roots*, and Joy Clarkson's *You Are a Tree*.

because there is no one-size-fits-all formula in the Bible for how to delight ourselves in the Lord because He created *us* one of a kind. And what works in one season of our lives will need to be tweaked in the next.

That's why I've chosen to use the terms *Rhythms of Delight* and *Rhythms to Restore Joy* interchangeably throughout this book, to remind us that just like waves ebb and flow in a rhythmic pattern, these practices shift and change as we grow and our life circumstances evolve. What doesn't change is that Jesus remains at the center of our lives as we practice these rhythms, and His delight in us calls forth our delight in Him. As "deep calls to deep" (see Psalm 42:7), so the Spirit of God reaches out toward us and calls us deeper into His presence.

All the Rhythms of Delight begin and end with love. They're an invitation to relationship, to joy, to completeness, to rest, and to abide in Jesus' love. We'll cover at length the following five rhythms that I've found central in my own journey of joy with Jesus:

- **Worship:** delighting in the heart of God through all we say and do

- **Word:** delighting in the revelation of God through Scripture

- **Whisper:** delighting in communion with God through prayer

- **Wonder:** delighting in the gifts of God by recognizing His hand at work

- **Walk:** delighting in obedience to God as we collaborate with His Spirit

These five rhythms have profoundly shaped the way I move in the world and the way I experience God's presence with me, even in seasons of brokenness, busyness, and burnout. And as these rhythms have become a natural movement of my day, sunrise to sunset, from season to season, God has expanded my capacity for joy.

## Brains Created for Joy

As we've already seen, joy is God's very good idea and His very good gift to us—but that doesn't mean we should ignore or suppress distressing emotions like anger, sadness, grief, or fear. Instead, we can bring these hard emotions to God and ask Him to help us process them, to understand where they're coming from, and to draw us closer to Him.

As we regulate our emotions with Jesus, our brains return to a state of peace and joy, which improves our behaviors, our relations, and our physical health (better sleep, better cardiovascular health, and better metabolism).[3] In other words, our bodies and our brains function best when fueled by joy, according to psychologist Allan Schore.[4]

True joy is *usually* relational, and our experience of joy expands when it's shared with others, almost like it's contagious. My friend Hannah's infectious laugh makes me smile just thinking of it. Relationships transform fleeting pleasure into lasting joy, and that joy can expand beyond the present moment when we relive happy memories or anticipate joy to come, like when we think back on a crisp autumn evening with friends around a fire, experience a loving embrace with our spouse, or look forward to a beach vacation with our family.

3. "How Do Thoughts and Emotions Affect Health?," University of Minnesota, Earl E. Bakken Center for Spirituality and Healing, 2016, https://www.takingcharge.csh.umn.edu/how-do-thoughts-and-emotions-affect-health.
4. "Allan Schore: Joy & Fun," YouTube, July 11, 2011, https://www.youtube.com/watch?v=Y0iocZu1mVg.

Why am I sharing all this? Because *relational joy* forms the foundation of these Rhythms of Delight that refocus our attention on our relational God. He indwells us in His personal way every moment of our day, and He restores to us His joy even as we process the hard aspects of life with Him because He created our brains with two wonderful aspects.

I first encountered many of these ideas in Marcus Warner and Chris Coursey's book *The 4 Habits of Joy-Filled People*, which I recommend if the brain science of joy interests you. Further research has made me realize what an expansive field brain science really is; I'm sure we'll discover more in the years to come, which only makes me more excited to learn how God wired our brains for joy.

## Our Brain's Joy Center

While many parts of our brain work together to process emotions, the region most often associated with happiness lives behind our right eye, in the right frontal cortex.[5] To help you picture this, place your right hand just above your right eyebrow, and remember that this is where your brain processes joy. Several scientists have called this our brain's "joy center" to keep it simple.[6]

Now get this: when a baby is born, their brain's Joy Center is barely developed, but it quickly grows thanks to mirror neurons in their brains that learn by watching and imitating the adults who hold them. All that cooing and awwing and smiling when you

5. Heidi Moawad, MD, "How the Brain Processes Emotions," *Neurology Live*, June 5, 2017, https://www.neurologylive.com/view/how-brain-processes-emotions.

6. I first encountered this term in Warner and Coursey's book (page 39), but in my research, I found the term used as early as 1994 in this *Washington Post* article: Don Oldenburg, "Headed for Pleasure: Pete Sanders and His Joy Touch Technique," September 30, 1994, https://www.washingtonpost.com/archive/lifestyle/1994/09/30/ideas/64a701a3-7a96-42e0-879b-bca46e0f8a27/.

hold a baby in your arms? It's scientifically proven to grow and expand their Joy Center, as babies' brains respond to the "sparkle" they see in grown-up's eyes with increased natural opioids.[7] And truly, when you see a baby smiling back at you, doesn't your own brain light up with joy?

What if the same can be said about our relationship with God? As we "fix our eyes on Jesus" (Hebrews 12:2), gazing upon the "sparkle" of delight in His eyes, our own hearts respond with joy—not just spiritually, but physically too! While I've never been hooked up to an MRI machine while fellowshipping with the Lord, two studies in 2008 and 2018 scanned the brains of monks while in a state of deep meditation. These brain scans showed "significant" increased activity in the brain's right hippocampus, leading to "long-lasting changes" in the "brain's networks"—in other words, the monks' brains actively changed *while meditating,* specifically in their Joy Centers and Joy Pathways (more on this in the next few pages).[8] Our brains literally light up with natural opioids when we encounter God through these rhythms He uses to restore our joy! Maybe this is what David was poetically describing in Psalm 34:5 when he wrote, "Those who look to him are radiant with joy; their faces will never be ashamed" (CSB).

Did you catch that? When we look to God, our faces will radiate joy, because we're reflecting the sparkle in our heavenly Father's gaze. Much like Moses' face reflected the radiance of God's glory,

7. H. S. Hoffman, "Imprinting and the Critical Period for Social Attachments: Some Laboratory Investigations," in M. H. Bornstein, ed., *Sensitive Periods in Development: Interdisciplinary Studies* (Hillsdale, NJ: Lawrence Erlbaum Associates Publishers), 99–121.

8. IEEE Signal Process Mag, 2008 Jan 1; 25(1): 176–174, doi:10.1109/msp.2008 .4431873, https://www.ncbi.nlm.nih.gov/pmc/articles/PMC2944261/.

so we too can begin to "radiate with joy" as we spend time with Jesus, speaking to Him "face to face, as one speaks to a friend," like Moses did (Exodus 33:11). Every time we say "yes" to delighting in Jesus, He's literally rewiring our brains and restoring our joy.

**Jesus can renew your mind by creating new synaptic connections that expand your capacity to receive His joy.**

Joy is always relational—it's often communicated through our gaze of affection and our loving attention. This Joy Center commands our emotional regulation and develops patterns of living with joy and returning to joy even after we encounter upsetting situations.

And while our Joy Center has been shaped in our childhoods, God designed our brains to continue growing and changing as long as we live. This amazing truth, called *neuroplasticity*, means that our brains can grow our capacity to experience joy even now, no matter our age. When we process the pain, hardships, or suffering we experience with Jesus through these rhythms that restore our joy, He gradually expands our Joy Centers—which can grow to fill up nearly a third of our brains.[9]

That's incredibly good news! Even if you've always been an anxious person, or a grumpy person, or an angry person, Jesus can renew your mind by creating new synaptic connections that expand your capacity to receive His joy. Which brings us to the second amazing brain discovery.

9. "How Do Thoughts and Emotions Affect Health?," University of Minnesota, Earl E. Bakken Center for Spirituality and Healing, 2016, https://www.takingcharge.csh .umn.edu/how-do-thoughts-and-emotions-affect-health.

## Our Brain's Fear Center

Just as we have a Joy Center, our brains also have a "fear center."[10] When we encounter robbers of delight that steal our joy, our brain functions from the back of the brain, the amygdala, located at the top of our spine. Place your right hand at the bottom of your skull. That's where the amygdala is located. God created our amygdala with a good purpose—it controls our response to perceived threats, flooding our bodies with the hormones necessary to flee from danger. This is a good thing. But we're not supposed to live in this state of constant alertness to danger.

Many of us are crippled by anxiety these days, an emotional state resulting from the constant chatter between a number of different brain regions, essentially creating a "fear network."[11] But God wants us to return from that fight-or-flight state back to a place of peaceful rest, and that's where Joy Pathways come in.

## Our Brain's Joy Pathways

God created the different neurons in our brains to communicate with other neurons through synaptic connections. What's fascinating is that each neuron can be connected to just a few other neurons or to thousands of other neurons. The more often these neurons communicate with each other, the stronger and

10. "Fear center" is my own term, naturally growing out of the context and the two other terms to describe the amygdala, brain stem, and limbic region of the brain, often called the "primitive brain" in scientific literature. In recent years, there's been research that all the areas of the brain work together to experience emotions, but certain parts that "light up" more than others during certain emotions. That's why I'm choosing to use the oversimplified term of "fear center" for this experience.

11. Elizabeth I. Martin et al., "The Neurobiology of Anxiety Disorders: Brain Imaging, Genetics, and Psychoneuroendocrinology," *The Psychiatric Clinics of North America* 32, no. 3 (2009): 549–75, doi:10.1016/j.psc.2009.05.004.

thicker their synaptic connection becomes. In plain English, that means the more often you do something, the easier and faster it is to do it.

It's these neurological pathways that help us navigate from up-setting situations back to a place of joy and peace. Authors Marcus Warner and Chris Coursey use the term "joy pathways," which I like because it's easy to envision these highways leading from the Fear Center in our amygdala to the Joy Center in our right pre-frontal cortex.[12] It's not that we'll never feel afraid, anxious, bored, or broken again. It's that we learn rhythms that bring us back to a centered place of joy with Jesus. And the more we practice these rhythms, the stronger our Joy Pathways will grow.

I also appreciate the term Joy Pathways because it brings to mind one of my favorite verses in the Bible:

> You make known to me the path of life;
> in your presence there is fullness of *joy*;
> at your right hand are *pleasures* forevermore.
> (Psalm 16:11 ESV)

Right now, I'm teaching my five-year-old to ride his bike. Do you remember what that was like? At his age, I was terrified I was going to fall over. But as I practiced pedaling and balancing, falling and getting back up again, I eventually learned how to ride a bike. And the more I rode, the more confident I became, until I was pedal-ing to school across cobblestone streets in Romania, then rushing down Austrian mountain roads on my honeymoon, and eventually pedaling up Ohio's hills during my first triathlon. Those early years learning to ride my bike created synaptic connections that grew

---

12. Again, I'm borrowing language from Warner and Coursey's excellent book, *The 4 Habits of Joy-Filled People*, 40.

stronger and faster, allowing me to face larger challenges and experience greater gains.

Becoming a stronger cyclist didn't shield me from other challenges: I've fallen off my bike many times; I've towed children behind me in a trailer; I've ridden in rain and cold. But each challenge provided opportunities to learn and grow and become a more resilient rider.

In similar ways, as we practice these Rhythms of Delight with Jesus and with our community, these Joy Pathways will grow stronger and more resilient. When we find ourselves in the Fear Center of our brains (as we inevitably will), we lean on these Rhythms to travel the Joy Pathway back to our Joy Center. Eventually, these neural pathways become so well-established that they're like highways in the brain, allowing signals to speed through up to one hundred times faster than other parts of our brains.[13]

When we return from the Fear Center to the Joy Center, we learn—even *feel*—what the psalmist means when he says in Psalm 23:1–3:

> The LORD is my shepherd; I shall not want.
>> He makes me lie down in green pastures.
> He leads me beside still waters.
>> *He restores my soul.* (ESV)

Riding the Joy Pathway back to the Joy Center of our brains, you'll develop habits that make joy a more regular, predictable part of your daily life, restoring your soul. Over time, you'll be able to recover joy more quickly, the process becoming more natural, just like riding a bike.

---

13. Tim Newman, "What Is Myelin?," *Medical News Today*, August 9, 2017, https://www.medicalnewstoday.com/articles/318966.

The reason I share all this is to give you hope: while God works to restore our joy spiritually, He also works physically (in our brain chemistry), emotionally (in our affect regulation), and mentally (in our cognitive behavioral patterns). We are not doomed to live out the rest of our days in burdens, brokenness, and burnout—God can indeed restore our joy, and He's already given us everything we need for that work of restoration to begin. We just need to learn to partner with Him in ways He's already revealed to us in Scripture.

## The Wonder of Brain Science in Scripture

We serve a creative God who invites us to connect with Him in creative ways. God welcomes us to come to Him whatever this season of life looks like, and the good news—the great news—is that He actually created our brains with the ability to form new habits no matter how old we are or no matter how many times we've failed before.

We see the kernels of habit formation early in God's call to the Israelites to be His people:

> Hear, O Israel: The LORD our God, the LORD is one. Love the LORD your God with all your heart and with all your soul and with all your strength. . . . Talk about [these commandments] *when you sit at home* and *when you walk along the road, when you lie down* and *when you get up.* Tie them as *symbols on your hands* and *bind them on your foreheads. Write them on the door-frames* of your houses and on your gates. (Deuteronomy 6:4–9)

I'd read this passage dozens of times over the years, but as I learned the science of habit formation, I recognized the crossover between what "experts" recommend and what God commanded His people all those millennia ago.

God didn't explain the science of habit formation or joy restoration when He instructed His people at Mt. Sinai. He simply told them what to do, already knowing how our human brains work. They simply had to obey Him in love to reap the benefits of what we now call *neuroplasticity*.

This is great news if we've struggled to be consistent in our Bible habits over the years because God can help us break bad habits and form new life-giving habits. You don't have to understand the science to benefit from this amazing gift of God.

As we practice a "new normal" under the guidance of God's Spirit, we're actively *crucifying the flesh* and *walking in the Spirit*, so that we can enjoy Jesus without fighting so hard to be consistent. Because we are embodied creatures, our physical brains play an important role in the spiritual transformation that we long for.

This is a big part of what Scripture means when it tells us to *renew our minds* (see Romans 12:1–2). As we practice these Rhythms of Delight, God's Spirit changes us, and our brains create new synaptic connections that make abiding in Jesus, resting in His love, and enjoying His presence part of our daily lives. And the more we practice these rhythms, the more naturally they fit into our lives, until it feels like they've always been a part of our walk with Jesus.

## Rhythms That Weave into Our Natural Movements

Notice in Deuteronomy 6 how God instructed the Israelites to talk to their children about His commandments while they did other normal daily things, like "when you sit at home" (like during a family meal), "when you walk along the road" (like when driving to soccer practice), "when you lie down" (like tucking in your kids at night), and "when you get up" (like getting the family ready for the day).

Brain science supports this approach of linking new habits to something we already do, making it easier to practice our new habit by making it visible and memorable. James Clear, author of *Atomic Habits*, popularized the notion of "habit stacking," but acknowledges that he got the idea from Stanford professor BJ Fogg's "anchor habits." In any case, they all describe linking up habits in a chain action sequence, which makes every habit easier than the one before it.[14] We'll cover specific examples in the chapters to come, but for the sake of illustration, here are some simple ways friends have woven rhythms into their daily movements:

- While showering, a friend practices memorizing a chapter of the Bible printed out and placed in a Ziplock bag that's taped to the shower wall.[15]

- A reader in our community listens to my *Prayers of REST* podcast while driving her children to school and starts their day together in prayer.

- Instead of checking social media while standing in line, another friend pulls up a verse memorization app on her phone and spends those 90 seconds reviewing Scripture.

The possibilities are endless, and the combination you come up with will be personal to your unique daily schedule and will likely change from one season of life to the next. That's okay. In fact, it's more than okay—that's the point. As you weave these rhythms of delighting in Jesus throughout your day, you'll find

14. James Clear, "How to Build New Habits by Taking Advantage of Old Ones," https://jamesclear.com/habit-stacking.

15. Glenna Marshall, *Memorizing Scripture: The Basics, Blessings, and Benefits of Meditating on God's Word* (Chicago: Moody Publishers, 2023), 44.

yourself more aware of His presence with you every step of the way.

For each of the Rhythms of Delight you'll read in the chapters to come, I'll encourage you to write down: "**What daily routines can I link to my new tiny habit?**" Try phrasing it this way: "When I _____, I will _____."

## Devotional Personality Types and Our Rhythms of Joy

Some Rhythms of Joy come more naturally to some of us than they do to others, and that's okay. Over the years of working with thousands of Christians around the world, I've learned that people feel close to God in different ways. I first heard Pastor Gary Thomas present this idea of "sacred pathways" to connect with God in his book by the same title.

Pastor Gary Thomas describes these personal differences as follows:

> Please don't be intimidated by others' expectations. . . .
> [God] created you with a certain personality and a certain
> spiritual temperament. God wants your worship, according
> to the way he made you. . . . In fact, by worshiping God
> according to the way he made us, we are affirming his work
> as Creator.[16]

Intrigued, I developed a "devotional personality quiz" and posted it on my website in 2017. Studying the quiz results of more than 40,000 readers, I realized that the top five "personality types" actually align with the five Rhythms of Delight I'd been studying sepa-

16. Gary Thomas, *Sacred Pathways: Discover Your Soul's Path to God* (Grand Rapids, MI: Zondervan, 2002), 17, 19.

rately. Both objective data and reader emails affirm that each of us has one primary rhythm of delight, one way we best sense God's presence. (Curious what yours is? You can go to www.delightingin jesus.com/book-resources to take the 90-second quiz.)

One rhythm is not superior to the others, and I've found that all five rhythms enrich our enjoyment of God's presence. I'd suggest you start with the rhythm that comes most naturally to you, and then work the other four rhythms in over time. It may take some intentionality, but with practice, they can all become movements we weave into our day to delight in Jesus.

We serve a creative God who made us to connect with Him in creative ways. How might He strengthen our Joy Pathways if we learned Rhythms of Delight that fit our devotional personality types: Worship, Word, Whisper, Wonder, or Walk?[17] Here are some examples:

If you're a naturally outdoorsy person, get outside with God—after all, the heavens declare His glory (see Psalm 19:1). Read your Bible on your front porch while watching the sun rise, or go for a prayer walk through the forest. Look forward to the feel-good hormones released in your brain that cheer you on: "This. This is how God made me to connect with Him!"

If you're a Bible nerd like me, block out an hour once a week to go deep on the geeky Bible resources available to

---

17. God created our brains to seek pleasure and avoid pain, so when our habits are enjoyable, we're more likely to stick with them. James Clear writes: "Habits are a dopamine-driven feedback loop. Every behavior that is highly habit-forming is associated with higher levels of dopamine." James Clear, *Atomic Habits: An Easy & Proven Way to Build Good Habits & Break Bad Ones* (United Kingdom: Penguin Publishing Group, 2018), 36.

you. A couple times a week, I sit down with concordances, dictionaries, Bible maps, and The Bible Project videos to delve deep into the world of theology. And in that place, I feel God's very presence.

**If you're an artistic person,** you may find great joy in coloring, painting, or hand-lettering your Bible study. I am not in the least artistic, but my daughters have enjoyed coloring key verses in the margins of their journaling Bibles while we take turns reading Scripture together.

**If you're a visual learner,** pull out highlighters and Bible-safe pens to mark up your Bible and prayer journal. I like to color-coordinate my study of Scripture, using different colors for different themes; it helps me stay more engaged while I read, and gives me a bird's-eye view of the frequency of those themes in each book of the Bible. You might also enjoy using charts (or drawing them yourself) to process the information you're reading.

**If you're a kinesthetic learner,** find tactile ways to enter into God's presence. Whether that's going for a prayer walk, dancing, using art supplies as discussed above, or even doing crafts that represent what you're learning or help you process your journey with Jesus, you might find the most enjoyment by incorporating movement into your rhythms of delighting in Jesus.

Create your own ideas to come into God's presence with "fullness of joy"—ideas that harness the power of your brain's dopamine to create rhythms of being with Jesus that prove to be "a joy" and "delight to [your] heart":

Your words were found, and I ate them,
and your words became to me *a joy and the delight* of my heart.
(Jeremiah 15:16 ESV)

## Celebrate Growth

Most of us recognize change in others, but we rarely pause to mark it in ourselves. Maybe we want to guard ourselves from pride; maybe we're so driven that once we've accomplished a goal, we're already tackling the next goal.

Whatever the reason, remember to pause and recognize where you're growing, and then celebrate that growth with Jesus: "I planted the seed, Apollos watered it, but God has been making it grow. So neither the one who plants nor the one who waters is anything, but only God, who makes things grow" (1 Corinthians 3:6–7).

If there's any growth in our lives, that's due to God's Spirit at work in us. He's the One who makes the seed grow and produce fruit. Why wouldn't we celebrate Him?

There's nothing prideful or arrogant in celebrating the good work God is doing in our lives. Think of Philippians 1:6—"He who began a good work in you will carry it on to completion until the day of Christ Jesus." As these rhythms become a natural part of the fabric of your life, God is transforming you into a person of prayer, a woman or man of the Word, a Jesus follower whose face radiates the joy of the presence of God. God is doing a good work in your life. That's worth celebrating! After all, it's scriptural:

Blessed are those who have learned to acclaim you,
who walk in the light of your presence, LORD.
They rejoice in your name all day long;
they celebrate your righteousness. (Psalm 89:15–16)

For each Rhythm of Delight in the upcoming chapters, consider how you'll reflect on and celebrate your growth with Jesus each week, month, and year.

## Are You Ready?

When you partner with God's Spirit to weave Rhythms of Delight into your daily life, you'll be delighted by all the ways He surprises you along the way. Over time, you'll naturally move through these Rhythms of Joy, ebbing and flowing as you have more or less time, coming back to delighting in Jesus throughout the hours of your day. Your Joy Pathway will grow stronger and faster, and you'll find yourself bouncing back from your Fear Center to your Joy Center, living out the psalmist's declaration:

> He brought me out into a spacious place;
> he rescued me *because he delighted in me.* (Psalm 18:19)

In it all, remember to keep your heart centered on Jesus. He is the reason for all these rhythms. He is the One our hearts long for, so may the action itself never eclipse our Beloved who's waiting for us to come and be with *Him.*

Yes, there will be days (perhaps many, many days) when we don't feel like it, when our hearts seem far from Him, but we keep showing up because of the promise of His presence. *He* is our reward; it's Him our hearts long for. And when our rhythms reinforce our affections, spiritual formation and transformation soon follow. Your neural pathways will form deeper and deeper grooves, and these rhythms will become as natural as breathing itself.

But guard yourself from falling into the trap of making the spiritual activity *the goal.* The goal is delighting our souls in Jesus . . . how we get there is just a rhythm of movement.

# CHAPTER 5

# Delighting in the Heart of God: *Worship*

I have decided to follow Jesus," we sang in joyous procession as we marched the cobblestone streets toward the closest river.

Typically, in the Romanian villages surrounding my own, the only parades through the streets headed toward the graveyard: somber gatherings of black-clad mourners led by a priestly figure, a golden cross, and a nailed coffin.

But this day's boisterous procession was led by Romani people who had exchanged their colorful garments for white clothes that day. We all sang at the top of our lungs, accompanied by musicians and accordions, attracting the curiosity of onlookers, many of whom would join the procession to see our destination.

These public baptisms were my favorite part of being a missionary family to the Romani, an ethnically distinct people group despised by most of our relatives and church acquaintances but dearly loved by God. The field was ripe for the harvest, and in the ten years of my childhood and adolescence that we served there, hundreds of Romani received the good news with great joy: Jesus had come to save not just the white Romanians but the neglected and downtrodden Romani as well.[1]

My childhood was filled with stories of drunkards turned preachers, daily bread miraculously provided, tons of clothing and food delivered, illiterate children graduating high school, and shocking racial reconciliation. God's Spirit moving in powerful ways during those pioneer years of ministry profoundly marked me and thousands of others.

"Though none go with me, still I will follow," I sang along with my new teenage brothers and sisters in Christ. We'd already shared our testimonies of how God had called us to Himself, and we were now ready to publicly follow Jesus into the waters of baptism.

I stood in the cold rapids, water swishing around my white dress as I looked out on the multitude covering the grassy shore. My father, clothed in his baptismal garments and flanked by two Romani pastors who were baptizing their own children that day, gripped my hands in one of his. His other hand rubbed circles on my back.

"Do you believe in Jesus as your personal Savior?" he asked, his eyes warm with affection.

"I do," I responded, hoping my voice carried over the waves to the onlookers on shore.

"Because of your faith in Jesus," he continued, "I baptize you in the name of the Father, and of the Son, and of the Holy Spirit." He

---

1. Parts of this narration are excerpted from my blog post "The Story I Didn't Want to Tell You (But I'm Sharing Anyway)," *One Thing Alone*, Summer 2015, https://onethingalone.com/the-story-i-didnt-want-to-tell-you-but-im-sharing-anyway/.

tipped me back, and I noticed the cloudless blue sky just before I shut my eyes and caught my breath. I heard the muffled words, "buried in the likeness of His death . . ." as cold waters enveloped me, but I felt no fear, knowing that my father's strong arms held me tight. Then he pulled me back toward the surface and into the sunshine, declaring ". . . raised to new life in the likeness of His resurrection."

Joy flooded my soul as I imagined my heavenly Father's pleasure even as my earthly father hugged me. My new church family on shore erupted in joyous song and celebration, and I stepped against the current to return to their embrace, my heart echoing the words, "No turning back, no turning back."

## Made to Worship

We tend to think of worship as the singing that happens in church on Sunday mornings. Some of us enjoy that more than others, and it's easy to dismiss worship as something a worship team does.

Frankly, for many of us, the thought of an eternity in heaven where all we do is "worship" this way doesn't sound very appealing at all. We may chuckle at the cartoonish image of angels sitting on clouds strumming their harps, and abstractly know that's probably not what God has in store for us, but in the absence of a more robust vision of worship, it's hard to replace that

> For those in the kingdom of God, all of life is sacred, and all of life is worship.

with anything more meaningful. After all, if we as humans were created to worship God, does that mean heaven is one long praise and worship concert? If so, some of us aren't going to want to leave an earth that's filled with breathtaking beauty, funny friends, and meaningful work.

But the biblical view of worship is actually much broader and encompasses all of life, not just the singing parts. Because there is *no* secular-sacred divide. For those in the kingdom of God, all of life is sacred, and all of life is worship.

## Our Very First Mission

To properly understand worship, we need to recapture a biblical understanding of who we are, and why we've been placed on this earth.

As the daughter of missionaries, I was caught up in the evangelistic zeal of the '80s and '90s, and nearly every church service I attended in the US circled back around to the Great Commission; that is, our call to make disciples who make disciples, to be on co-mission with God. For much of my childhood, the Great Commission shaped my understanding of who I am and what God has called me to do.

It wasn't until my early thirties that I was challenged to consider the Great Commission in light of our First Commission—that is, the mission given to our ancestors, Adam and Eve, in the garden of Eden: "God blessed them, and God said to them, 'Be fruitful, multiply, fill the earth, and subdue it'" (Genesis 1:28 CSB).[2] Before the fall, before sin entered the world, God created humans in His own image and blessed them to harness creation's potential and nurture beauty and order in the world. Because God created us in His own image (see Genesis 1:26), He's given us the divine privilege to represent His rule on earth.

---

2. I first encountered this language of the "First Commission" in light of the "Great Commission" as "The Unabridged Gospel" in my friend Jordan Raynor's *The Sacredness of Secular Work* (Colorado Springs: Waterbrook, 2024), chapter 1. It's a great book. You should read it.

Bible scholars Tim Mackie and Jon Collins of The Bible Project explain in their conversational way that in biblical times, kings considered themselves divinely appointed to rule as gods:

> These kings would often make statues of themselves, which in Hebrew were called *tselem*, often translated as "idol" or "image." But for Israel, they didn't view their kings as the god. In fact, they were never supposed to even make images of God . . . because God has already made images of himself . . . [when] surprisingly, as the pinnacle of all of God's creative work, he makes humans. And he calls all of them the "image of God." . . . So he gives all humans the authority to rule.[3]

This divine privilege is essential to what it means to be human, given to us as our first co-mission with God; and while the history of humanity shows we've stewarded this divine privilege poorly, Jesus is our new Adam, the image of the invisible God, fully God and fully human.[4]

In His earthly life, Jesus showed us what it looks like to truly live out this commission to serve and love as a human, and His Spirit fills us with divine power to transform us into this new humanity that reflects God's image to the world and moves His kingdom forward, on earth as it is in heaven.[5] I know this might feel like some deep theological weeds, but stick with me here, because I promise it all comes together to reveal a beautiful picture of delighting in Jesus through worship.

---

3. Tim Mackie and Jon Collins, "Image of God," The Bible Project, Mar. 21, 2016, https://bibleproject.com/explore/video/image-of-god/.
4. See Romans 5:12–21; 1 Corinthians 15:22, 44–49; Ephesians 1:10; and Colossians 1:15–17.

## God's First Priests

While the First Commission to image God by representing His rule of the world applies to all humans, those of us who follow Jesus and belong to His family have an additional call on our lives: that of priests on this earth.

In the ancient world's understanding, a priest was a person who represented their deity's power and reign to their nation, and also represented their nation to their deity. They did this by offering sacrifices to appease their deity; seeking their deity's approval (or lack thereof) of important decisions like marriages, alliances, and wars; and coordinating their nation's celebration of the deity at feasts and festivals. All of this was the priest's duty and privilege of worship. (I, for one, am grateful we don't have to go through with bloody sacrifices anymore, aren't you?)

In the biblical understanding of the world, there is no god other than Yahweh. All other pagan worship is empty, devoid of power and influence. But those who worship the Lord have access to the one true God, the Creator of the world, the King of the universe. Starting in the garden of Eden, both Adam and Eve were endowed with this holy priesthood responsibility of representing God to creation and creation to God.[6] Eden was the place where heaven overlapped with earth, and God walked with the pair in the cool breeze of the evening.[7]

5. I'm deeply indebted to The Bible Project's entire body of work to reframe my perspective on Genesis 1–3, specifically their videos on the book of Genesis, https://bibleproject.com/guides/book-of-genesis/.

6. For more on how God intended for Adam and Eve to represent Him as royal priests, see The Bible Project's video "Royal Priests of Eden," https://bibleproject.com/articles/were-adam-and-eve-priests-eden/.

7. If you want to learn more about the garden as temple imagery, read Dr. J. Daniel Hays's *The Temple and the Tabernacle: A Study of God's Dwelling Places from Genesis to Revelation* (Baker Books, 2016).

Sin, of course, marred this perfect worship, as we see as early as Genesis 4, where Cain misses the heart of worship, and offers an unacceptable sacrifice. But God was not far from him: "If you do what is right, will you not be accepted?" (Genesis 4:7). We see this same invitation to do what is right in worship to the one true God threading throughout Genesis and into Exodus, as God chooses one family, which becomes one nation, to reveal Him to the world.

At Mount Sinai, shortly after rescuing His people out of slavery in Egypt, the Lord invites them into a covenant to become a kingdom of priests to the nations, to show them what God is like, and into a restoration of His presence among them, but they refused (see Exodus 20:18–19).[8] They received the Law as a tutor in "what is right," but the privilege of priesthood was then placed on only a select group of the Israelites, the Levites. And so they served as priests throughout Israel's history, up until the day of Jesus.

## A Kingdom of Contemporary Priests

Jesus came to fulfill the Law, and through His life, death, and resurrection, He birthed a new kingdom of holy and royal priests:

> You yourselves . . . are being built to be a holy priesthood to offer spiritual sacrifices acceptable to God through Jesus Christ. . . . You are a chosen race, a royal priesthood, a holy nation, a people for his possession, so that you may proclaim the praises of the one who called you out of darkness into his marvelous light. (1 Peter 2:5, 9 csb)

Did you catch that?

Those who belong to Jesus are being shaped into a holy priesthood, a kingdom of royal priests who proclaim the wonder of our

---

8. See also Exodus 19:5–6.

Savior to the world, and the burdens of our world to our Savior. Our First Commission to represent God's rule on earth is now empowered by His own Spirit.

But our lives as priests in the twenty-first century look very different from the responsibilities of our Jewish counterparts. We don't offer bloody sacrifices on an altar made of stone because Jesus, the Lamb of God, fulfilled the need for those sacrifices. No, our sacrifice, our worship, is much different: "Therefore, brothers and sisters, in view of the mercies of God, I urge you to present your bodies as a living sacrifice, holy and pleasing to God; this is your true worship" (Romans 12:1 CSB).

A sacrifice is something you give over as no longer your own, a gift to a deity that usually involves killing a sacrificial animal. We're urged to present our bodies as a living sacrifice, but God does not desire our physical death; rather, He calls us to life to the full—a mode of living every moment as an offering to our heavenly Father. And this sort of sacrifice is "holy and pleasing" to God—it brings Him pleasure and enjoyment to watch us live into the fullness of life He created us for. Not just watch us, but actually empower us to live this way (see Hebrews 13:20–21).

## More than a Song

How we live, how we work, how we parent, how we eat, how we love, how we play, how we make out or make up . . . it's all worship. Or, it can be, if it's offered as a gift to the One who made us and delights in us. Our worship is our response to the One who loves us, and our lives lived as a gift to God is our delight in the heart of God.

That doesn't mean that we sing our way through our day like we're trapped in some sort of musical. Worship invites awareness of our actions, attitudes, and aspirations—becoming more intentional in every area of our lives. We worship as we present our embodied living as a living sacrifice, which brings a smile to our heavenly Father in His good pleasure. Delight responds with delight, an unending rhythm of giving and receiving.

We embody our commission as God's representatives on earth when we plant a flower garden to beautify our front yard, when we make room at the table for those who are lonely and alone, and when we make time to listen to our next-door neighbor's concerns about the proposed tax levy. We embody our liturgy when we sing praises at the top of our lungs in the church sanctuary, when we weep at hospital bedsides, and when we cry out for justice for the oppressed. We embody our role as priests in the world when we check out at a grocery store, when we present a PowerPoint at work, and when we kiss a boo-boo on our child's knee.

> All of life becomes worship when we delight in the light of God's presence.

All of life becomes worship when we delight in the light of God's presence. It doesn't have to be complicated. Brother Lawrence offers this simple approach as "little acts of interior adoration" invisible to the world. He says, "A little lifting up of the heart suffices; a little remembrance of God, an interior act of adoration." This can be done in the midst of life, as we "think of God as much as possible so that [we] will gradually become accustomed to this little but holy exercise."[9]

We learn these rhythms of restoring joy by looking at the life of Jesus. "All of Christ's action is our instruction," according to Thomas Aquinas; so let's turn our attention to the Gospels to see how Jesus lived out this rhythm of worship.

---

9. Brother Lawrence, *The Practice of the Presence of God* (Ada, MI: Baker Publishing Group, 1967). Kindle, 24.

# CHAPTER 6

# Practicing Jesus' Rhythm of Worship

Shortly after my father left, I found myself in that dry wilderness again, now a new mother but still desperate to experience God's closeness once more.

"Why don't You hear me?" I'd ask Him in prayer. "Why don't You answer me? Why is my Bible reading so dry and boring? Come back into my life!"

That fall, I'd attended a women's conference at my church, and emailed the speaker, Linda Dillow, whose love for Jesus and joy in His love were absolutely contagious.

"I used to be joyful too," I lamented. "How do I get it back?"

"The path into face-to-face intimacy," she said, "is to bask in the presence of God through worship. Worship is not just a specific act. It's also a lifestyle."

It was then that I realized that despite my years growing up in church, serving on the mission field, and launching a devotional

> Our sense of God's nearness to us comes not from what precisely we do in worship, but rather from opening ourselves to encounter Him in worship.

blog . . . I didn't know how to worship. Not really.

Linda was kind enough, amid her busy schedule, to not just email me but mail me a copy of her book *Satisfy My Thirsty Soul*, and the first three chapters were like a glass of cold water for my parched heart. I wrote in my journal that evening: *Truly I don't really know what worship looks like outside of a corporate setting. But You, Father, know. Teach me and guide me over the next twelve weeks into deeper intimacy with You, as I learn to worship in private and through my entire life.*

In the resources Linda sent me, she writes:

> Worship begins in holy expectancy that we will see God, and it ends in holy obedience. The specific act of worship—bowing my knees in holy expectancy—has taken me into the presence of God and true intimacy. The lifestyle of worship—bowing my life in holy obedience—has taken me to a new level of living faithfully for Christ. . . . Worship is the lifestyle of a grateful heart.[1]

I learned that our sense of God's nearness to us comes not from what precisely we do in worship, but rather from opening ourselves to encounter Him in worship.

---

1. Linda Dillow, *Satisfy My Thirsty Soul* (Colorado Springs: NavPress, 2007), 27–28.

# Jesus' Rhythm of Worship as a Model

If our lifestyle of worship is bowing our lives in holy obedience, Jesus' entire thirty-three years spent on this earth were lived in pure and pleasing worship to His Father. We don't have to do a keyword-search on the word "worship" in the Gospels to recognize this rhythm of delighting in the heart of the Father, because it's interwoven throughout Jesus' life.

**Jesus perfectly worshiped in spirit and truth, and we can model our own rhythms of worship on His.**

We also get a fly-on-the-wall peek into Jesus' conversation with a Samaritan woman on the topic of worship, which reveals that our misconception of worship as a bullet point in the weekly church service is as ancient as the temple: the Samaritan woman too wanted to know the technicalities of where and how and what of a proper worship service. Jesus refocuses her on the more important part of worship: not the location or the music genre, but the heart.

> "But an hour is coming, and is now here, when the true worshipers will worship the Father in spirit and truth. Yes, the Father wants such people to worship him. God is spirit, and those who worship him must worship in Spirit and truth." (John 4:23–24 CSB)

The Father is seeking people who will worship Him in spirit and truth. Jesus perfectly worshiped in spirit and truth, and we can model our own rhythms of worship on His.

## Jesus Participated in Worship Services

As a faithful Jew, Jesus attended regular worship services at the local synagogue (see Luke 4:16) and at the temple in Jerusalem, where He observed the religious feasts as prescribed in the Law. These feasts included singing and dancing, reciting Scripture and prayer, and while the Gospels don't record the specifics, as a faithful Jew, Jesus would have fully participated in all these religious activities.

Many of us who have grown up in church have inherited a robust tradition of worship in our own church services. As Linda's book reminded me, worship is so much more than just mumbling the lyrics of the song led from the front of the stage—it's offering our singing, our prayers, our presence as a sacrifice of "spirit and truth," like the priests of old used to do with their animal sacrifices.

Sometimes, when I'm gathered with our local congregation on Sunday mornings, I close my eyes and picture our voices raising up to God's throne room, the sound waves undulating like the smoke of incense in His presence (see Psalm 141:2; Revelation 5:8 and 8:3–4). I don't entirely know what this means in theological terms, but I do know that it's part of our work as priests and part of the reason we're told to continue gathering with the local body of Christ. Whether the musical style is my personal preference or not is secondary to whether my heart is open and united with my spiritual siblings in adoring our heavenly Father.

## Jesus Sang as Worship

Scripture records that Jesus sang hymns (see Mark 14:26, likely a musical rendition of Psalms 113 to 118), and as an observant Jew, He would have known and sung all the songs of their custom, including the jubilant Psalms of Ascent when walking up to the temple courts. Imagine: the Word of God, who inspired David to write these psalms, then gave voice to them as He sang the songs He helped pen. What would it have been like for Him to join in the chorus of voices singing in harmony?[2]

> Hallelujah! Give praise, servants of the LORD; praise the name of the LORD. Let the name of the LORD be blessed both now and forever. From the rising of the sun to its setting, let the name of the LORD be praised. (Psalm 113:1–3 CSB)

Worship is so much more than singing, but it's not less than singing. Singing has a way of both expressing emotions and forming our theology, and sometimes it can draw our attention back to the heart of God ever so subtly, even without our realizing it.

## Jesus Rested as Worship

We don't tend to think of rest as worship, but the Lord made it clear when He gave His people the rhythm of resting on the seventh day, that it was intended to train their hearts in worshiping Him (see Exodus 16:22–30). The newly liberated people had to learn to trust God to provide for them, and Jesus demonstrated this dependence both in His wilderness testing (see Matthew 4:3–4) and in His complete trust that His Father would care for Him, like when He fell asleep in a boat in the middle of a storm (see Matthew 8:23–27). Jesus fulfilled the Sabbath not through rigid abstaining from work, but by demonstrating that He truly understood the meaning and purpose of the Sabbath.

We too can learn to rest as worship, whether it's by keeping a Sabbath day in our weekly rhythm, or identifying the places in our lives where we hustle for meaning, identity, and significance

---

2. On that note, I wonder if His voice is a tenor, bass, or baritone. These are things I can't wait to find out when I finally see Him face-to-face!

and surrendering those to Jesus. We can learn rhythms of rest in our daily, weekly, monthly, and yearly lives.

## Jesus Worked as Worship

While most of the gospel accounts focus on Jesus' three years of public ministry, He spent the majority of His life in relative anonymity, working a day job like everyone else.

When we embrace work as a means of worship, we learn to receive work as a gift from the hand of God and do our jobs (as little or as large as they may be) as if doing it for our heavenly Father. Viewed thus, our work, whether vocational or voluntary, becomes a way we partner with God's creative energy in the world, advancing His vision here on earth as it is in heaven, a spiritual act of worship.

## Jesus Performed Miraculous Works as Worship

Fully God and fully human, Jesus embodied His role as the perfect human, the new Adam, with all the implications of image-bearing and priestly work from Genesis 1-2 brought to the forefront. This brings fresh meaning to Jesus' words:

> "My Father is still working, and I am working also.... Truly I tell you, the Son is not able to do anything on his own, but only what he sees the Father doing. For whatever the Father does, the Son likewise does these things." (John 5:17, 19 csb)

> Then they took away the stone from the place where the dead man was lying. And Jesus lifted up His eyes and said, "Father, I thank You that You have heard Me." (John 11:41 nkjv)

While few of us could claim miraculous works as part of our resume, all of us who belong to Jesus are indwelled by His Spirit, and we're invited to co-labor with Him in the good work He's doing in the world, the good works He prepared beforehand for us to walk in (see Ephesians 2:7–10).[3] So in God's kingdom, even giving a cup of cold water in Jesus' name is received by Him as worship, an act of embodying God's love here on earth.

## Jesus Adored and Surrendered to His Father as Worship

Throughout His earthly ministry, Jesus exuded adoration for His Father, from the intimate "Abba" opening in the Lord's Prayer to how He lived at one with the Father, doing only that which His Father gave Him to do.[4] Jesus perfectly embodied a life of adoration and surrender to His Father's will.

Imagine Jesus singing the words of this psalm, included in the Passover tradition called Hallel, during the Last Supper:

> I will take the cup of salvation
> and call on the name of the LORD.
> I will fulfill my vows to the LORD
> in the presence of all his people.
>
> The death of his faithful ones
> is valuable in the LORD's sight.
> LORD, I am indeed your servant. (Psalm 116:13–16 CSB)

This took place mere hours before He would obediently walk into His arrest, trial, and crucifixion. These words would have been the soundtrack in His mind as He prayed in the garden that night, "Father, if you are willing, take this cup from me" (Luke 22:42).

---

3. See also Matthew 11:25–26 and Mark 8:6 in giving thanks for the bread before multiplying it for the multitudes and Mark 14:23 in giving thanks for the cup.
4. See Matthew 6:9–13, Luke 11:1–4, and John 5:17–18.

See the imagery carrying over? Jesus knew exactly what that "cup of salvation" from Psalm 116 would entail: "the death of his faithful one." Notice Jesus' costly worship here in His prayer of wrestling and surrender: "Yet not my will, but yours be done." If ever there was costly worship, it was there. Complete surrender.

As we follow in Jesus' footsteps, our own lives will mirror this dynamic of adoration and surrender. As we grow in deep love, respect, and devotion to the Father, we will progressively surrender more and more of our lives to Him, in total and complete trust, learning to say with Jesus, "Not my will, but Yours be done." This too, done in spirit and in truth, is an act of worship pleasing to the Father.

The entirety of Jesus' life could be summarized as worship "in spirit and in truth." As the "new and better Adam," Jesus came to fulfill what our ancestors failed to do, living the life of a perfect human, a perfect priest, a perfect co-ruler with God, thus inaugurating His coming kingdom among us, inviting us to join Him in His reign as a "kingdom of priests," "a royal priesthood," "a holy nation" (see Exodus 19:6 and 1 Peter 2:9–17).

What does this rhythm of delighting in the heart of the Father through worship look like for us today?

## Creative Ideas for Worship Rhythms in Daily Life

In the spring of 2015, after emailing Linda and receiving her book, I followed her advice and began setting aside ten minutes several days a week to worship. I'd put on some music, ask God to lead me, and kneel before Him (not just metaphorically, but actually getting down on my knees). I read Psalm 63 over and over and declared to God all the truths I discovered about Him: who He is, what He has done, how majestic He has revealed Himself to be. And then I'd lapse into silence, until the ten-minute timer went off. Some days, more words would arise that I wanted to tell Him; other days I got restless and kept checking the timer. Some days I'd practice being present in the moment, and just being quiet before God, while other days I sensed Him whispering something to my heart.

When the timer went off, I'd take a deep breath and reenter my day, carrying with me an awareness of God's loving presence. I tried to picture Him with me while driving to work, writing reports, and eating my lunch. I reminded myself of His presence while picking up groceries, cuddling my baby, and folding socks. Because I'd grounded myself in the reality of His presence earlier in the day, it made practicing His presence that much more natural during the rest of my activities.

I still think back on those weeks with fondness, not just because I was hesitatingly practicing a new rhythm of worship, but also because I can trace much of the fruit of my ministry back to those early days of encountering God face-to-face. Time in God's presence changed me, and that change trickled into the lives of my family, my church, and my online ministry community.[5]

---

5. My very first book, *Full: Food, Jesus, and the Battle for Satisfaction*, was born out of these sessions of quiet worship and surrender. The introduction explains how God's Spirit met me in one of these times of worship and led me on a life-changing journey that has now, through His power, helped thousands of readers. By His mercy and grace, God meets us in our weakness, comforts us in our brokenness, heals our diseases, and uses for good what the enemy intended for evil. I'd forgotten this connection between the beginning of my worship journey and the beginning of my food freedom journey until I was writing this chapter. That God would not just meet me in this secret place of worship but also grow the seeds planted in those private moments into fruit that reaches women around the world? It blows my mind. He is so kind. So powerful. And His plans are far beyond our own. We need only to come with open hearts; He will do the rest—exceedingly, abundantly, surpassingly more than we could ask for or imagine.

Eight years later, at a church breakfast for volunteers, an elderly woman came up to me and said, "I first met you when you led that Bible study on worship Wednesday nights."

"Oh, yes," I replied with a huge grin. "I didn't know if anyone would show up." A year after my own worship awakening, I couldn't keep this experience to myself, and I invited the women of my church to join me in reading the book and worshiping together. To my surprise, the room was packed each week. It was then that I realized I wasn't the only one who thirsted for more of God—many others sitting in pews each week did too.

"You were pregnant with your second child, and every week your baby bump would get bigger and bigger, but you'd still get down on your knees with us to worship," said the woman. "I thought, 'I don't know if she'll be able to get back up this time. But if she's doing it eight months pregnant, I'm doing it too.'"

We shared a laugh at that. I remembered the precarious balancing act of trying to get back up on my feet those evenings.

"But do you know?" she continued. "I kept getting down on my knees every day to worship the Lord, all these years, until I had a hip replacement last spring and now I can't anymore. I miss those days when I could kneel down before Him; but now I just sit in my chair as I worship Him, and it's still the best part of my day."

She beamed as she said those words, the joy of Jesus shining bright on her face, and I felt a pang of sorrow. I had stopped that practice after my labor and delivery, and in my sleep-deprived fog, I simply hadn't picked it back up. There was no physical limitation keeping me from kneeling but simply my own comfort. It was time to begin again.

That is where I invite you to begin, where I began (and re-began) all those years ago.

## Kneeling in Worship

For the next six weeks, in the privacy of a set-apart place, commit ten minutes a day to worshiping God for who He is. For many, first thing in the morning works best, but adapt this experience to your current season and needs. It could be ten minutes of your lunch break, or ten minutes in the carpool line, or ten minutes before bed. Simply find a time and place where you won't be interrupted.

Here are some suggestions:

**Put on some music in the background.** I find quiet instrumental works best because my mind is prone to wander.

**Get down on your knees if you're able.** Consider kneeling on a pillow, if needed. (The point isn't to be miserable but to posture our body in a way that mirrors the inner posture of our hearts.) If you really can't kneel, like my church friend, find a comfortable position that still communicates bowing before God, perhaps by bowing your head.

**As you worship, ask God to teach and lead you.** Expect Him to answer your request.

**Read a psalm out loud.** Psalm 63:1–8 is where I started, but you can start with your favorite psalm and read on from there. At first, you may feel awkward reading to an empty space, as I did, but with practice you'll find your voice.

**Remember that God is present with you.** You're talking to Him, so ask Him to open your eyes to see His wonder in His Word.

**Declare God's goodness based on what you read.**[6]
What does the text say about who He is? What He's done?
Consider how these truths about God have been revealed
throughout the biblical story, throughout the world's
history, and throughout your own life's story as well.
Remember, you're not praying to sound good to anyone;
you're learning to communicate affection to the One who's
worthy of all your adoration. Here's what I have said, based
on the first verse alone; your declarations of worship will
be different and personal to you:

- You are my God. Ever since I was a kid, You drew me to
  Yourself.
- You make Yourself available when I seek You. You don't
  play hide-and-seek with me. How kind You are.
- You are the water of life who satisfies my thirst. And You
  invite me to come.
- You created me for Yourself, and it's only in You that I
  find true fulfillment.

**Be quiet with God when you've run out of things to
say.** After all, we're not trying to impress Him with how
much we can squeeze out of a few verses. And any healthy
relationship leaves room for two-way communication. Ask

---

6. If you want a guided prayer and worship experience based on Scripture, I've written 365
   prayer prompts in my book *Prayers of REST: Daily Prompts to Slow Down and Hear God's
   Voice* (Chicago: Moody Publishers, 2022). I still marvel at the far-reaching ripple effects
   that first season of worship has had on my personal life and writing ministry. I share this
   because God eagerly waits to work powerfully in your life too. You may not see the fruit of
   your worship encounters for years to come, but make no mistake: God is reshaping you to
   be His priest here on earth, fit for the good works He has prepared for you, and it will be a
   beautiful thing to watch unfold for years to come.

God to quiet you with His love, and rest in the assurance that God hears you, He loves you, He receives your worship, and He's surrounding you with His own love and delight.

**Tell Him whatever else comes to mind.** If you get distracted in your stillness by some random thought, don't ignore it—tell God about it, declaring His goodness even in that situation, and then return to a place of quiet rest.

**Record His responses.** Sometimes, in these moments of stillness, God's Spirit will whisper something to your heart. He might bring to mind a specific person who needs prayer. Or maybe a promise from Scripture that speaks to a current struggle. Or an idea for a problem you've been wrestling with. Whatever He speaks, write it down (either in your journal or in the margin of your Bible, along with the date) so you can remember and act on whatever He gives you. You'll also create a record of His faithfulness to look back on over the years.

**Carry the assurance of God's presence with you.** Do this throughout the rest of the day. Once the timer goes off, your worship continues in everything you say and do.

## A–Z Worship

Another way to delight in Jesus through worship is by bringing an awareness of His presence with us throughout our day and growing our vocabulary for worship. Sometimes I find myself repeating the same words or phrases, bored with my own words. Surely the God whose creativity crafted the Amazonian rainforests and Arctic wilderness and Andes mountains can teach us both variety and beauty in the way we worship Him.

One way I've learned to do this is by worshiping Him from A–Z, thinking of fun or unique names or attributes of God for each letter of the alphabet. This too I learned from Linda Dillow and practiced not only with my Wednesday evening worship group at church but also at church retreats I lead and speak at. It's a simple, fun worship experience alone or with others:

1. Quiet your heart with a few songs. Again, I prefer relaxing instrumental here.

2. Kneel, walk, or even grab a dry erase marker to write on your windows. Embrace your unique learning style here (visual, auditory, kinesthetic).

3. Begin with the letter "A" and tell God everything you appreciate about Him that begins with that letter. Then move on to the letter "B," and so on. (If you get stuck on a letter, it's okay to get creative, skip a letter, or check my ABCs in this book's resource library at www.delightinginjesus.com/book-resources.)

4. Reflect on your time of worship when you've finished the alphabet. What did you learn (or remember) about Him? How did the experience affect you? Was it easy or hard, fun or challenging? Which letters' worship response most surprised you? Record a few thoughts in your journal or the margins of your Bible.

## Morning Worship Playlist

One of the ways I set the tone for my day is by starting my morning with songs of adoration and praise. I've cycled through different playlists, sometimes leaning heavily on English and Romanian hymns, other times welcoming the contemporary beat of modern songs, and most recently creating my own playlist of songs that direct my heart to delight in Jesus (find my Spotify playlist at www.delightinginjesus.com/book-resources). When I find my heart weary or prone to wander, I pull up the playlist and let the melody and lyrics direct my heart back to the Father in worship. **Do you have a rotation of favorite songs that refocus your heart on Jesus? Consider creating a playlist of your own, or print out the lyrics and put them in a binder to come back to again and again.**

## Congregational Singing as a Sacrifice of Worship

I've attended many churches over the years due to my family's travels and missionary work, and the singing ranged from stoic Baptist hymns to chart-topping contemporary songs; from somber songs written in minor keys by Romanian Christians imprisoned for their faith, to an upbeat Zulu tune that had us swinging and clapping and praising at the top of our lungs.

Not every church service's music will appeal to us. That's okay. The music isn't for us, not really. These melodies of worship are meant for God, after all. We're just the officiators of the worship, the ones who, as priests, offer to Him a "sacrifice of praise" that, when offered prayerfully, rise to Him as pleasing incense (see Hebrews 13:15–16, Psalm 141:2, and Revelation 5:8 and 8:3–4). And in the singing, we actually benefit too in ways that scientists are only beginning to discover.[7]

---

7. An article in *Time* magazine explains that "group singing has been scientifically proven to lower stress, relieve anxiety, and elevate endorphins." But scientists acknowledge they still have much to learn on this topic. Stacy Horn, "Singing Changes Your Brain," *Time*, August 16, 2013, https://ideas.time.com/2013/08/16/singing-changes-your-brain/.

This coming Sunday, join your church in congregational singing, and as you do, imagine yourself as a priest, bringing a physical offering to God's throne room. As the sound waves fill the room, picture them rising to God's heavenly presence as smoke would rise to the skies. (If your church uses smoke machines, this exercise is even easier.) Lift your hands in worship as a priest would lift up a sacrificial animal to the Lord (after all, that's the gesture we're imitating, did you know?).

Pay attention to the lyrics, and whisper to God additional words of worship based on your private time of worship during the week. (You might notice repeated names of God or verses between your private and corporate times of worship; these are not "coincidences"—they are God's personal nudges to remind you that He sees your worship in secret, and He's rewarding you with a more personal knowledge of Himself. See Matthew 6:6.) You may even feel prompted to sit or kneel in response to the congregational worship—follow the Spirit's prompts as He leads you in this time.

As we reframe congregational singing as less about us and more about a joint priestly activity, we begin to see that those twenty minutes of worship were never really about us, how we feel, or our musical preferences. It's about God's people coming together to declare their adoration, their trust, and their delight in their Creator—all together once a week before we go our separate ways to continue that worship throughout the week.

## How Will You Delight in the Heart of God?

As we wrap up this chapter, consider how you can begin practicing this rhythm of worship in your own life. **Pick one of the creative**

**worship ideas above, or come up with your own. Then make an action plan to make it a natural part of your life.**

- How will you make this Rhythm of Worship small?

- What daily routines can you link to your worship? "When I _____, I will _____."

- How can you make your Rhythm of Worship fun and personal to you?

- How will you celebrate your growth each week? Month? Year?

Remember that we're not creating a checklist—we're creating new pathways of delighting in Jesus. If you find yourself resisting your rhythm of worship, ask yourself if you've forgotten the reason for this. How can you recapture the sense of Jesus' presence with you as you worship Him? Can you imagine Him kneeling next to you? Can you picture Him seated on His throne, smiling at the congregational sacrifice of praise? Can you see Him pleased with your creative worship and giving you ideas when you're stuck on a letter of the alphabet?

As much as we desire to delight in Jesus, He longs for us so much more. And one of the primary ways He reveals Himself to us is through His Word, to which we turn next.

CHAPTER 7

# Delighting in the Revelation of God: *Word*

Growing up in a Romanian family, Sundays were for feasting. My mom and I would regularly prepare three-course meals consisting of a bone broth-based soup, pasture-raised braised meat, roasted veggies fresh from the garden, and multilayered pastries that melt in your mouth. If you left the table feeling anything less than stuffed, you were doing it wrong.[1]

Maybe in your family it's Saturday morning pancakes or Friday night pizza, or maybe you didn't grow up with a family feasting

---

1. This emphasis on fellowship around the table in a culture of abundance was part of what led to my food fixation and struggle for freedom years down the road, which I chronicle in my book *Full: Food, Jesus, and the Battle for Satisfaction* (Chicago: Moody Publishers, 2016).

tradition but you'd like to start one with your own family—we all intuitively know that something special happens when people linger together over good food and delicious drinks. It's what friends and families have done for millennia.

It's also the metaphor Jesus uses when describing His desire for friendship in Revelation 3:20: "Here I am! I stand at the door and knock. If anyone hears my voice and opens the door, I will come in and eat with that person, and they with

> We hustle through our days spiritually malnourished and emotionally frazzled, forgetting that Jesus stands at the door, patiently waiting for us to invite Him in.

me." Here's a picture of leisurely enjoying one another's company, sharing stories and hopes with each other, and growing to know one another over time. What a beautiful invitation to life and friendship with Jesus.

Jesus invites us to delight in Him, to get to know Him, and to share our heart with Him, even as He shares His heart with us. And the way He reveals His innermost thoughts and desires with us is through His Word—the daily bread offered by the Bread of Life for our daily nourishment (see Matthew 4:4).

Unfortunately, we hustle through our days spiritually malnourished and emotionally frazzled, forgetting that Jesus stands at the door, patiently waiting for us to invite Him in.

## A Broken Systematic Approach to Bible Reading

The Word of God has been written down for us, made readily accessible to us. And the Word of God is alive in us, readily available to us. He wants to offer us more of Himself, His own Spirit, and abundant life in Him—it's all ours for the taking if we would just sit with Jesus through the reading of His Word.

Sadly, many religious leaders have turned Jesus' invitation of mutual revelation into a daily obligation, stripping this rhythm of Bible reading of its delightful nature and turning it into a "spiritual discipline" that reveals only how dedicated a person is to their religious practice. Meanwhile, we miss out on the fellowship and friendship God offers us in Jesus.

How many of us feel guilty that we don't read our Bible more? Even people in full-time ministry confess that they struggle to increase their Bible reading, as though information input alone can change us.[2]

We have more access to the Bible through the technology available at our fingertips, yet over the past five years, Bible reading dropped dramatically, from 49 percent in 2019 down to 38 percent in 2024.[3] According to American Bible Society's 2024 State of the Bible report, generational trends lean toward less Bible reading, less loving interactions with God and others, and less Bible-based decision-making:

- 24 percent of senior citizens regularly engage with Scripture

- 12 percent of Millennials regularly engage with Scripture

- 11 percent of Gen Z adults regularly engage with Scripture[4]

2. Ted Olsen, "How to Jump Back into Bible Reading," *Christianity Today*, February 15, 2019, https://www.christianitytoday.com/ct/2019/march/how-to-jump-back-in-to-bible-reading.html.

3. American Bible Society, *State of the Bible 2024*, https://1s712.americanbible.org/state-of-the-bible/stateofthebible/State_of_the_bible-2024.pdf, 3.

4. Ibid., 11.

We know that God's Word is important, and many of us make plans to read it more, especially around the New Year. But while 84 percent of American Christians make a goal to read their Bibles more, only 15 percent actually increase their reading year over year.[5] Interestingly, even when the overall Bible reading percentage decreases, respondents still claim their Bible reading increases. According to the report writers, "This probably indicates that people want to think they've been reading the Bible more, whether or not they really have been."

Did you think you were the only one to fall off your reading plan mid-Leviticus? Nope, it's not just you. The way we've been taught to approach Bible reading as a spiritual discipline is simply not working.

Maybe it's time we question the "quiet time formulas" we've inherited, and instead ask God to help us develop new rhythms of being in His Word—rhythms that deepen our love for Him rather than deepening our guilt over arbitrary reading goals.

## An Embarrassment of Riches

We have this precious gift, God's own Word written and recorded and preserved for us, so that we would never wonder what God wants to say to us. It's all written here, a record of who He is, what He has done, and what He has promised for those who trust in Him—a feast waiting to satisfy our deepest longings.

For hundreds of years, only the educated few could access the carefully transcribed and illuminated Latin Scriptures. Millions of churchgoers relied on their local priests and pastors, doing their best to honor God without once holding the Bible in their

5. Ibid, 4.

hands or reading God's Word in their own language.

My own great-grandmother, Măicuța, grew up in communist Romania and didn't own a Bible until she was married. In her village, they'd pass around single pages of the Bible and read them, transcribe them, and memorize them before trading the pages with another. The scarcity of the written Word of God made it all the more precious. And if they were caught with pages of the Bible in their homes, they risked beatings, imprisonment, and harsh labor.[6]

The Romanian community I grew up in had living memories of people who had endured these punishments because they cherished their Bibles. Even knowing the risk, they continued to read God's Word, memorize it, and share it with anyone who would listen.

My dear friend Silvia Tărniceriu spent years in a Romanian prison, locked up for her faith and deprived of her Bible. For four months she was systematically brainwashed and mentally tortured until she couldn't remember *a single verse* of the hundreds she had memorized during her childhood. In her darkest moment, she cried out to God asking for a verse—any verse—to bring her comfort in her suffering. He responded with a whispered *Love your enemies*. At first, Silvia resisted, hoping for a promise or a psalm; but when none came, she obeyed the Spirit's prompting the next morning, cheerfully greeting the prison guard who had mistreated her.

The next moment, Psalm 23 flooded to her mind: "The LORD is my shepherd, I lack nothing. . . . Even though I walk through the

---

6. And all this with only a second-grade education. Măicuța lived with us for a couple years when I was an adolescent, and I still can picture her holding her little personal Bible in her hands, her finger tracing the page as she worked to decode each word letter by letter. Reading never came easily to her, but she never stopped trying until the day she died, at age ninety-two.

darkest valley, I will fear no evil, for you are with me." Silvia writes in her memoir:

> My memory was back! I clasped my hands together! I could clearly remember everything! I was free! Oh, I cannot tell in words the freedom that came over my soul. I was no longer in prison! My spirit was free in Christ! . . . I could not stop praising God, and I could not stop quoting verses. Songs came back. I laughed and cried. I had to keep on working, but I could not keep from singing. "There's no other friend like Jesus," I sang. I could not keep silent. A well of joy was flowing from me.[7]

God's revelation of Himself through those verses so marked her that as soon as she was released from prison, Silvia spent the rest of her life touring the globe, raising awareness for the persecuted church. Her blue eyes sparkled whenever she spoke of her friend Jesus, up until the day she went to be with Him in 2013.

Corrie ten Boom, who had also been imprisoned for her faith and obedience to Jesus, is credited with offering this maxim: "Gather the riches of God's promises. Nobody can take away from you those texts from the Bible which you have learned by heart."[8] Such was certainly true for Silvia in that Romanian prison, as it's been for many others persecuted throughout history.

But fast-forward to today, and we seem to have forgotten the treasure we hold in our hands. No other generation in the history of humankind has had unlimited access to the Word of God at

---

7. Harvey Yoder, *God Knows My Size—Silvia Tărniceriu,* (Berlin, Ohio: TGS International, 1999), 208.
8. This specific quote is widely attributed to Corrie ten Boom but isn't directly found in any of her main published works.

their fingertips—and for all that, we are living in the most biblically illiterate generation since the Reformation. By choice. As Eric Geiger, vice president of LifeWay Resources, aptly put it: "Here in the US, the problem isn't that people don't own a Bible. It's that they don't read the Bible they have."[9]

But if your Bible's collecting dust on a shelf, Silvia would be the first to tell you: there is no condemnation for those who are in Christ Jesus (see Romans 8:1). Instead, God's compassionate Spirit convicts us to turn toward Him in repentance, that He may stir up our hearts and restore our joy.

## Stir in Me a Holy Hunger

Jesus, the Bread of Life, offers Himself to us each time we open the pages of our Bibles. So, let us turn our gaze from the distractions that promise to fill us but only leave us empty, hungry for something of substance that will satisfy. As John Piper writes:

> If you don't feel strong desires for the manifestation of the glory of God, it is not because you have drunk deeply and are satisfied. It is because you have nibbled so long at the table of the world. Your soul is stuffed with small things, and there is no room for the great. God did not create you for this.[10]

I first read this quote about ten years ago, and I remember realizing the truth of those words. I lacked an appetite for God's Word

---

9. "Lifeway Research: Americans Are Fond of the Bible, Don't Actually Read It," Lifeway Research, April 25, 2017, https://research.lifeway.com/2017/04/25/lifeway-research-americans-are-fond-of-the-bible-dont-actually-read-it/.

10. John Piper, *A Hunger for God: Desiring God Through Fasting and Prayer* (Wheaton, IL: Crossway Books, 1997).

because I had been stuffing my soul with insignificant trifles: social media posts, entertaining shows, captivating novels, and delicious entertainment. Honestly, none of these things were sinful or morally ambiguous. They would all pass the test of "would you watch/read/do this thing if Jesus were watching?" But what these activities had in common was that they took up most of my free time and satiated my spiritual appetite so that I never really hungered for God's Word.

It was God's own Spirit who convicted me that these things were keeping me from delighting in God's Word, causing me to miss out on a deeper revelation of His heart. He was the One who led me to lay them down for a season, with the prayer that God would awaken in me a spiritual hunger like never before. Day after day, I'd show up to my open Bible with the same heart cry: "Stir in me a hunger for Your Word, Lord."[11]

Is there something in your life that's keeping you from hungering for God's Word? **Take a moment to sit in quiet reflection with God's Spirit, and write it in the margins to come back to later.**

## Reading the Bible, but Missing Jesus

Several weeks into my multi-sensory fast, as I wove the rhythm of fasting with the Rhythm of Worship and this rhythm of reading God's Word, it finally clicked for me: "The Bible isn't about me. And it's not an instruction manual either. The Bible is one big story that points to Jesus. And it reveals God's mission to bring

---

11. I write extensively about this season of fasting from sugar, from TV shows, and from novels in my first book, *Full: Food, Jesus, and the Battle for Satisfaction* (Moody, 2016).

us back into eternal communion with Him, to delight in Him forever and ever."

I'd been reading Jen Wilkin's book *Women of the Word* in conjunction with my daily Bible reading, when I underlined this quote:

> We must make a study of our God: what he loves, what he hates, how he speaks and acts. We cannot imitate a God whose features and habits we have never learned. We must make a study of him if we want to become like him. We must seek his face.[12]

I'd acquired a lot of Bible trivia in my years as a pastor's kid and later a missionary kid; I knew a lot about God, but I wondered if I was growing to become more like Him. The decade that followed my father leaving saw a steep rise in breaking news reports about evangelical leaders' public failings, entire blogs and podcasts dedicated to uncovering hidden sins. Each story felt like a fresh betrayal, triggering the same wound: *How could people who know the Scriptures so well live so poorly?* Too many church leaders boasted a robust knowledge of Scriptures but failed to live a life of sacrificial love, and I feared I would become one of them. I was afraid of becoming a hypocrite, a religious person who knew a lot *about* Jesus but failed to *live like* Him because my heart felt far from Him.

I lived in real fear that I would be like the Pharisees, to whom Jesus said: "'You study the Scriptures diligently because you think that in them you have eternal life. These are the very Scriptures that testify about me, yet you refuse to come to me to have life'" (John 5:39–40).

---

12. Jen Wilkin, *Women of the Word: How to Study the Bible with Both Our Hearts and Our Minds* (Wheaton, IL: Crossway, 2014). Kindle, 190.

What a chilling accusation. These teachers of the Law knew their Hebrew Bible better than anyone, but they didn't see that every word pointed to Jesus. The Word became flesh and made His dwelling among them, and they missed Him!

How often I also have missed Jesus in my reading of Scriptures. How often I've approached the Word as a *thing* to read while missing the *Person* waiting to offer Himself in its pages. The truth, proclaimed loudly throughout the Bible, is that God desires to reveal Himself to us ever-increasingly through His Word, offered freely to all who would take time to meditate on it and therein discover infinite joys and delights.

Consider how Scripture talks about this all over its pages:

- "When your words came, I ate them; they were my joy and my heart's delight, for I bear your name, LORD God Almighty." (Jeremiah 15:16)

- "I rejoice in the way revealed by your decrees as much as in all riches." (Psalm 119:14 CSB)

- "[Blessed is the one] whose delight is in the law of the LORD, and who meditates on his law day and night. That person is like a tree planted by streams of water, which yields its fruit in season and whose leaf does not wither—whatever they do prospers." (Psalm 1:2–3)

- "Open my eyes that I may see wonderful things in your law." (Psalm 119:18)

- "No one has ever seen God, but the one and only Son, who is himself God and is in closest relationship with the Father, has made him known." (John 1:18)

These verses cast a vision beyond gaining head/intellectual knowledge about God's Word. Picture a deeper burrowing of God's Word into our hearts, into the very core of who we are, until all our desires, affections, hopes, and imaginations are shaped by God Himself. Imagine opening your Bible and hearing the whisper of your Good Shepherd speaking directly to you, and as you lean in to hear His voice, your heart leaps within you. That is a picture of delight. That is what God desires to offer us, through the Word made flesh and the Word on the page.

As theologian Graeme Goldsworthy explains, "The meaning of all the Scriptures is unlocked by the death and resurrection of Jesus."[13] It's through the life, death, resurrection, and reign of Jesus that all the Bible begins to make sense. As we read, study, and meditate on the life of Jesus recorded in the Bible, God Himself reveals His heart to us.

## No Longer Alone: God's Personal Revelation Through His Spirit

But let's be honest here: reading the Bible is not as easy as reading an email or text message. I wish it were. With modern communication, we often rely on context, on our knowledge of the sender's personality, and on cultural trends or emojis to help us interpret what they mean. But when it comes to the Bible, these helpful extras are often lost to us, and this ancient book becomes something of a mystery.

It's easy to become bored with our Bibles if we struggle to understand its foreign context. Even though the Bible was written for us, it wasn't written to us, and while its message of God's love for

---

13. Graeme Goldsworthy, *Preaching the Whole Bible as Christian Scripture* (Grand Rapids, MI: Eerdmans, 2000), 54.

us in Christ Jesus is simple to understand, that doesn't make it necessarily easy to study.

God is after our hearts, not our checklists. Knowing and loving Jesus grows us to become more like Him, not seminary degrees or biblical trivia. And we get to know Him by learning more about Him, with our minds and hearts and spirits engaged in the work.

And when we stumble on something we don't understand or doesn't make sense about God's character as revealed in Jesus? There's no need to panic. Instead, rejoice that God is about to teach us something new, something we haven't seen or understood before. Rest in the assurance that God wants to reveal Himself to us—far from being disappointed in our lack of understanding, He's thrilled with our desire to know and love Him more. For God looks upon the humble with favor, and He gives to those who ask for more of Him (see Isaiah 66:2 and Luke 11:13).

Even in this, Jesus has made provision for us; we don't have to wrestle with the text alone:

> "I will ask the Father, and he will give you another advocate to help you and be with you forever.... All this I have spoken while still with you. But the Advocate, the Holy Spirit, whom the Father will send in my name, *will teach you all things* and will remind you of everything I have said to you." (John 14:16, 25–26)

Jesus asked the Father to send us His own Holy Spirit to teach us and remind us and guide us as we read, meditate on, and study God's Word. How kind of the Lord. Oh, how He delights in our desire to know Him more through His Word, even if we bumble our way sometimes.

> "When the Counselor comes ... *he will testify about me....* *I still have many things to tell you,* but you can't bear them now. When the Spirit of truth comes, *he will guide you* into

all the truth. . . . He will glorify me, because he will take from what is mine and *declare it to you."* (John 15:26; 16:12–15 CSB)

Jesus foresaw our need for a personal guide through the Scriptures and sent His own Spirit to us. We don't have to struggle alone. As we open our Bibles each day and encounter a text we don't understand, ask God's own Spirit to lead and guide us deeper into the hidden things of God.

Not every reading of the Word will result in euphoric revelations, but continue with a daily rhythm of the Word anyway, confident that each nugget of Scripture is a deposit into the treasure chest of our hearts—and someday we will see its beauty, even if we don't yet understand it now. I love how Jen Wilkin describes this mindset shift:

> For years I viewed my interaction with the Bible as a debit account: I had a need, so I went to the Bible to withdraw an answer. But we do much better to view our interaction with the Bible as a savings account: I stretch my understanding daily, I deposit what I glean, and I patiently wait for it to accumulate in value, knowing that one day I will need to draw on it.[14]

God's own Spirit will teach us all things, so there's no need to feel discouraged when reading the Bible is hard. Instead, trust that as we spend time with the Word made flesh—with Jesus—while studying the printed Word on the page, He will reveal the Father's heart to us through His Spirit's work in us.

---

14. Wilkin, *Women of the Word*, 105.

## Leaning into Our Need for a Guide

As God revealed to me His personal desire and provision in this area, I began praying: "Holy Spirit, open my eyes that I may see wonderful things in God's Word. Help me delight in reading my Bible. Help me see and savor Jesus on every page. Show me the heart of the Father even in the parts I first find boring. Only You can do this."

And He did.

God's Spirit was so faithful to "guide me in all truth," to "glorify Jesus" by "taking what is His" and "declaring it" to me. I'd read a passage of Scripture and something would click—I'd see something wonderful about God I'd never seen before and feel a quickening in my heart.

When you read a verse that God's Spirit led you to as a personal answer to a prayer request, or when you make a connection between the Old Testament and the New Testament that unlocks a grander picture of Jesus, your soul soars with worship, doesn't it?

These revelations aren't just for us. We share with one another what we've learned through the Spirit's revelation.

It's the excited text messages telling our friend, "You'll never believe what God showed me in my Bible reading this morning!"

It's the coffee shop conversation that prompts you to share with a tearful friend the verse you just read—you *know* God gave it so that you could pass it on to her.

It's the practice of coming together to study Scriptures in community and celebrating how each person sees something different in the text, a different facet of God's character that reveals His brilliance, like twirling a diamond in the light.

As we shift from immediately asking "How does this apply to me?" to first asking "What does this say about Jesus?" our head knowledge moves into our hearts. Bible information leads to heart adoration and then life transformation, or else reading the Bible is pointless. With this Rhythm of Joy—delighting in God's Word—both our heads and hearts encounter the beautiful divine in the pages of this ancient book. Our application will flow from adoration for who God is and what He's done. Because you can't spend time with Jesus and remain unchanged.

# CHAPTER 8

# Practicing Jesus' Rhythm of the Word

Wednesday evenings have become the highlight of my week, because on Wednesdays, we feast.

I'm not talking about a literal feast, though my friend Melissa usually has a magazine-worthy spread of scones and sparkling water on her kitchen island waiting for us. I'm talking about feasting on God's Word together.

For the last eight months, I've gathered with a small group of women every week to study God's Word in community, and every week I drive home riding a euphoric high. I feel like I've won the friendship lottery. These precious friends have become so dear to me as we've celebrated birthdays together and grieved the loss of loved ones together, laughed together and shed tears together and prayed together.

But at the center of our gatherings, what keeps us coming back week after week, has been the study of God's Word, the revelation of the heart of God.

These amazing women have modeled for me a genuine curiosity about the Scriptures, and a courageous tenacity, not just to dive into a difficult book (Exodus, not for the faint of heart), but to ask hard questions and sit with the tension of not having all the answers. After years of studying the Bible on my own, or just with my children in my home, it's been so good for my soul to set the spiritual table and invite friends to come, sit, and feast.

What amazes me every week is that we bring our meager loaves and fish, and Jesus multiplies our small offering to satisfy our hungry souls with the Bread of Life.

## Snacking and Feasting on Scripture

In our spiritual nourishment, we can develop rhythms of snacking and feasting on Scripture.

Most days, I come to the table of the Bread of Life early in the morning for a morsel of God's revelation that I meditate on throughout the day, energizing me for my work, until I pause again in a few hours for another snack of Scripture. Just as I don't expect one giant breakfast to fuel me all day, I keep coming back to the spiritual table of God's Word for nourishment.

But once or twice a week, I block out a couple hours to *feast* with Jesus, reading God's Word and letting it "read" me—receiving God's revelation of Himself through the pages of my Bible and also receiving His Spirit's gradual revelation of my own sin, my fears, my hopes, my innermost thoughts as I linger with Him at the table. I fill the margins of my Bible with notes, the pages with color-coded highlights, and my own journal with Scripture-saturated prayers and reflections.

It's in this place of quiet fellowship that I feel closest to Jesus, in those moments when He shows me something new about who He is and how wonderful the Father's love for us is. We sit together, me and my Bible and Jesus through His Spirit in me, and we delight in each other's presence. Few experiences can compare to the joy of being fully known and fully loved by the One who created you, gradually coming to know and love Him more and more. Better still are those gatherings when together we open God's Word and open our hearts and share what He's revealed to us.

I used to feel guilty that this experience, wonderful as it is, was not a daily occurrence anymore, not since my days as a teenager. Sometimes I long for the day when my house is once again quiet, my schedule once again my own, and I can feast with Jesus for hours each day. Until then, I'll take whatever moments I can with Him, even if it means weaving lots of Scripture snacks in my day.

So, how do we develop a rhythm of the Word in our daily lives? We find a perfect example in Jesus' own life, inspiring us toward creative ways to delight in God's revelation through His Word, even when these need to change from one season to the next. For all the suggestions below, you'll find recommended apps, links, and up-to-date discounts at www.delightinginjesus.com/book-resources.

## Jesus Listened to the Word

Before He could even speak a word, Jesus heard the Word of God in His family's Sabbath gatherings, in the synagogue's public readings, and in the psalms sung during community celebrations and laments. God's people were instructed to teach their children His Word from morning to evening, through their normal rhythms of life (see Deuteronomy 6 and chapter 4 on habit formation in Scripture).

Because printed Bibles are so freely available to us in the Western world, it's hard to imagine this, but as a poor carpenter, Jesus did not own His own personal copy of the Hebrew Bible. Papyrus, scrolls, and ink were so expensive and the copy work so laborious that these collections of God's Word belonged to the entire community, housed in the local synagogue and treated with the utmost respect.

Up until the invention of the printing press, few people in the world had their own personal copy of the Bible, so listening to the Word proclaimed in public gatherings and corporate worship became the primary way most people had access to the Scriptures. And for many people today, Sunday morning's reading of the text is still the most Scripture they get all week.

## Creative Ways to Listen to the Word

In the fall of 2013, when newborn exhaustion kept me from my regular Bible study rhythms, God's Spirit led me to listen to the audio Bible during my daughter's midnight feedings. Every night, multiple times a night, I'd get up to soothe my baby's cries, hit "play" on the Bible app, and let God's words wash over my weary soul for twenty to thirty minutes. I didn't realize just how many hours of a mama's life are spent feeding her baby until I'd finished listening to the entire Bible . . . in just four months.

I say this not as a humblebrag, but rather to express my own initial surprise that something I thought only spiritual giants can do (read through the Bible in a year or in just a matter of months), could easily be done by an exhausted person when interwoven into the rhythm of regular life.

Where in your schedule might you hit "play" on the audio Bible and let God's Word speak over your life?

## Jesus Learned the Word

In becoming fully human, Jesus took on all the limitations of human flesh, including needing to learn and memorize things just like the rest of us. Luke 2:41–52 shows Jesus listening to temple teachers and asking questions, ending with, "And Jesus increased in wisdom and stature, and in favor with God and with people" (Luke 2:52 csb). Jesus grew in His knowledge and understanding of Scripture, which means that as we work to learn the Word, we're following the way of Jesus.

We learn the Word by repeatedly exposing ourselves to it, whether by reading, listening, memorizing, or meditating on it. We learn the Word by familiarizing ourselves with its ancient context, using the myriad resources available at our fingertips, like study Bibles, commentaries, podcasts, and excellent videos. We learn the Word by sitting under the faithful expository teaching of the Word, which is a fancy way of saying verse-by-verse explanation, like in a Sunday morning sermon or in a theologically rigorous book.

## Creative Ways to Learn the Word

### Bible and Breakfast

A Chinese pastor once said, "No Bible, no breakfast." His commitment was to feed his soul before ever feeding his body, and the daily stomach growlings worked to motivate him to prioritize his Bible. While I appreciate the sentiment, as a busy young mom I needed a way to both read my Bible and eat breakfast.

So, I started "Bible and Breakfast." Every morning, I'd read a few verses from the Bible while my kids and I ate. This worked well when my kids were young and we enjoyed slower mornings together, but we've had to find new rhythms for our Bible time together that fit our changing schedules over the years, and that's okay.[1]

### One-Question Scripture Snacks

If you're new to Bible study, or if a deep daily inductive study isn't realistic for you right now, start with just one question after you read a short Bible text:

**What does this passage teach me about God?**

That's it.

This simple question focuses our attention on how God reveals Himself through Scripture, and if you write your one-sentence response to that prompt in the margin of your Bible, you'll soon have a record of how God gradually reveals Himself to you.

This one-question method is how I've been teaching my own children to read and interpret Scripture, and while I look forward to the day when I can introduce them to more advanced hermeneutical principles, for now, this first question is building a solid foundation for the rest of their lives. My own Bible is filled with scribbles in the margins from what my children are learning about God as we read through books of the Bible together, and I treasure those moments when their faces light up with a new insight into God's compassionate character.

If you have a few extra minutes, journal your responses to these three questions:

- What does this passage teach me about God?

- What do I want to say to Him in response?

---

1. Starting in 2015 and in the years that followed, over a thousand women joined us every fall for a 31-day challenge of Bible and Breakfast. If you're intrigued by this rhythm of the Word, why not try it for 31 days and see if it works for you? Learn more at www .bibleandbreakfast.com.

- What is God calling me to do now?

This "Scripture snack" is an abbreviated study when you're short on time, but the soul-satiating goodness comes when we make time to FEAST on God's Word too.

### FEAST on the Bread of Life

For those days when you can carve out extra time to linger at the table with Jesus, here's a simple inductive method that I've taught to thousands of women around the world. It uses the acronym FEAST to help us remember each part of the process.

#### Focus on God

Before you begin, take a deep breath and become aware of God's loving presence surrounding you and indwelling you through His Spirit. Ask Him to reveal Himself to you as you study His Word. I find it helpful to read a few verses of a psalm to center my heart and attention on Him.

#### Engage the Text

Next, read the passage multiple times, out loud if possible. Notice what words or phrases stand out to you. Is there any repetition, contrast, or comparison? Mark up the text with underlines, arrows, and circles. Answer the question, "What does the text say?" Embrace your learning style by listening to the audio Bible while you read, highlighting key phrases with fun colors, or acting out scenes with your children. Have fun as God's Spirit leads you into new discoveries about Himself.

## Assess the Meaning

After you've written your observations, it's tempting to jump straight into application, but hold off—we need to answer the question, "What does this text mean?" Even though the Bible was written *for* us, it wasn't written *to* us. We need to understand the culture, the context, and the literary genre to interpret the meaning for the original audience, keeping in mind that the Bible is one big story that points to Jesus. Read the surrounding context, study notes, and commentaries to learn about the book's purpose, audience, and cultural time period. Bible apps are great for this step.

## Spark Transformation

Now we're finally ready to ask God's Spirit, "What do You want to do in me?" This isn't about SMART applications or self-improvement plans; this is acknowledging that God grows us into the image of Jesus when we obey His prompts. So, we ask Him to spark transformation in our lives by showing us how to live in light of what He has revealed to us: "What is God calling me to do now?"

## Turn to God in Worship

I used to end my Bible study time by rushing off to apply what I've learned. But the ultimate goal of Bible study is not merely information or purely application but growing *adoration*. Spend time thanking God for who He is and what He has done, and then step into active worship as you walk empowered by His Spirit to love those He's placed in your life.

## Jesus Memorized the Word

As a Jewish boy, Jesus memorized the first five books of the Hebrew Bible by the time he'd turned thirteen. And we know He memorized it because when Satan tempted Him in the wilderness, He responded with verses from Deuteronomy (see Matthew 4:1–11). Throughout His earthly ministry, Jesus quoted the Law and the Prophets, as well as many of the psalms, showing that all of God's Word was hidden in His heart.

But remember: while fully God, Jesus was also fully human, so He had to memorize Scripture the same way we all do—through much repetition. If you've ever struggled with a bad memory and told yourself you just can't memorize God's Word, you'll be comforted to picture a ten-year-old Jesus repeating the same verse over and over again, missing a word here or there, until it finally settled into His memory.

Jesus knows memorizing Scripture can be challenging because He's experienced it too. He can empathize with our weaknesses, and we can confidently ask Him to help us in our Bible reading, study, and memorization (see Hebrews 4:15–16).

# Creative Ways to Memorize the Word

When my son was born, I'd gotten into the habit of checking Instagram every time I'd feed him. Hours and hours every day, wasted on pixels that offered temporary entertainment, only to leave me with a gnawing discontentment. Remembering my audio Bible experience with my daughter years earlier, I deleted the app and moved a Bible memorization app in its place. Our church's women were studying the gospel of John.

For decades I'd told myself I had a terrible memory, so I was surprised (and delighted) when I memorized the first eighteen verses—in just three weeks. But more important than the achievement of memorizing Scripture while dealing with brain fog and raging hormones, the presence of Jesus with me and my son became so real in those moments, and the miracle of His embodiment so personal, that His delight overtook my soul.

Perhaps you, like me, think you have a bad memory and won't be able to remember any verses you memorize. You'll be encouraged to know that perfect recitation isn't really the goal here. As pastor Andrew Davis writes:

> The point is not ultimately to be able to recite every verse perfectly, but to humbly and deeply saturate ourselves with the word of God. Regardless of what we eventually remember, the kind of meditation required for extended memorization will change us. That means no prayerful, meditative Scripture memory is wasted, even if we seem to have forgotten it all (and you won't forget it all).[2]

Here are some creative ideas to help you "hide God's Word in your heart" through memorizing it:

**Write the Word:** Write down the verse you're trying to memorize every day. As you slow down to transcribe the words, they'll slowly become ingrained in your mind and heart.

**Try the "first letter" method:** Rather than writing out every word, write down just the first letter of each word. Your brain will automatically recall the word associated with each letter,

2. Andrew Davis, "Why I Memorize Books of the Bible," Desiring God, May 21, 2021, https://www.desiringgod.org/articles/why-i-memorize-books-of-the-bible.

and it's faster to practice too. (I've penned the first letters on my wrist before, but you can find beautifully designed temporary tattoos to help you do this too.)

**Listen to the Word:** I've made a practice of listening to Matthew 5–8 over and over again, multiple times a week, in conjunction with my other memorizing tactics, with the goal of one day memorizing the entire Sermon on the Mount. I'm not there yet, but the more I hear the words, the easier my brain remembers their cadence and rhythm.[3]

**Make a "mind palace":** When I had trouble keeping the Beatitudes straight, I learned to create a mind palace, placing each blessing in a different part of my kitchen and living room. After only a few minutes of saying the Beatitudes as I physically walked through my home, I was surprised to find that I no longer confused the pairings or forgot their order. It worked!

**Sign the Word:** While helping my children memorize Psalm 23 and the Lord's Prayer, I started using hand motions, realizing that the kinesthetic movement helped both them and me remember the longer passage. Some of the signs are borrowed from American Sign Language, and some are made up by us, but all the same it's a fun way to learn ASL and Scripture at the same time.

---

3. For an up-to-date list of my favorite Bible apps that I use every day, as well as discounts on my favorite Bible resources, go to www.delightinginjesus.com/book-resources.

**Sing Scripture songs:** Talented songwriters have put Scripture to music, both for children and adults. I still remember many of the '90s Scripture songs my parents played in the car, and nowadays you can find many melodies composed for grown-ups too.

We can delight in Jesus as we work to memorize Scripture because, as Mark Bubeck writes in his book *Warfare Praying*, "When we memorize the Word of God, we actually put within our minds the mind of Christ. That Word becomes a helmet of salvation to the mind."[4] This is how we have "the mind of Christ" in us, by storing up the Word of Christ within us (see 1 Corinthians 2:16) and dwelling on it all day long.[5]

## Jesus Spoke the Word

As the Word made flesh, every word that came from Jesus' mouth was the inspired Word of God, so it goes without saying that Jesus spoke the Word. But by this I mean also that He explained God's Word to those who would listen, like when He showed His disciples on the road to Emmaus how every promise, every prophecy pointed to Him (Luke 24:27).

---

4. Mark Bubek, *Warfare Praying: Biblical Strategies for Overcoming the Adversary* (Chicago: Moody Publsihers, 2016), 152.

5. In the spring of 2023, while on a family trip to Romania, we visited an Eastern Orthodox church for a midnight Easter service, and I was shocked by how much Scripture was sung during its liturgy, covering the gospel story from Jesus' miraculous conception through His ascension and promised return. This challenged so many preconceptions I'd held about services in the Orthodox church; when I asked a priest the next week to tell me more about this, he explained that these New Testament excerpts are sung because music helps us remember, and they're repeated every week "so people would remember and meditate on the gospel all day long." What a beautiful example of corporate memorization through song!

How incredible it would have been to be a fly on their backpack, listening in on that Bible lesson. I look forward to the day when Jesus will explain how God fulfilled His promises through these recent millennia of human history. What a fun conversation that will be.

### Creative Ways We Can Speak the Word

In the meantime, Jesus' own Spirit lives within us, ready to teach and guide us in all truth. Not only that, but we get to join Jesus in the work He's doing when we share with one another what we're learning from the Word.

In our Wednesday night gatherings, we first read the chapter together, then discuss the following questions:

- What stood out to you in this week's text?

- What confused you?

- What did you learn about God?

- How does this text point to Jesus?

- How is God calling you to respond to what you learned?

Whether we're in the gospel of John, the book of Exodus, or following along with our pastor's sermon series, these lively discussions enliven our hearts and spur us on to deeper study as we see and savor Jesus together.

And we don't even need to have all the

> Sometimes, we have to sit in the tension of not knowing, leaving questions pending until the day comes when the Spirit will reveal the answer to us.

answers. Sometimes, we have to sit in the tension of not knowing, leaving questions pending until the day comes when the Spirit will reveal the answer to us. Often in my Bible reading, I'll draw a little question mark next to a passage, sometimes adding, "What are you doing here, God?" or "I don't understand this." And that's okay, because "Now I know in part; [but] then I shall know fully, even as I am fully known" (1 Corinthians 13:12). Even when we don't know the answers, we can trust the heart of God and rest in His perfect love and care for us.

## Jesus Prayed and Sang the Word

If you've grown up in a church tradition that values spontaneous prayers over scripted prayers, like I did, you might be surprised to learn that Jesus often prayed the psalms. The most obvious place we see this is when He cried out on the cross, "My God, my God, why have you forsaken me?" (see Psalm 22:1 and Matthew 27:46). In His most anguished moments, when Jesus had no other words to pray, the words of the psalms pour out from His heart.

While this might be the most clearly recorded instance in the Gospels, God's people used the Psalter as their prayer book throughout their week. For example, Psalm 92 features the super-script "A psalm. A song. For the Sabbath day," and is traditionally recited three times during each Sabbath.[6] The Levites would follow a weekly schedule of singing certain psalms for each day of the week at temple services, a rhythm followed by some Jews at morning prayer services at their local synagogues as well.[7] And faithful

6. "Reciting Psalm 92 Three Times," AskTheRabbi.org, https://www.asktherabbi.org/question/reciting-psalm-92-three-times/.
7. Each day's scheduled psalm correlated to the days of Creation, sung by Levites from ancient times and recorded to be sung by faithful Jews gathered in synagogues at least since the later part of the first century. In case you're curious, like I was, this weekly schedule was as follows: Sunday: Psalm 24; Monday: Psalm 48; Tuesday: Psalm 82;

pilgrims sang the Psalms of Ascent (Psalms 120–134) on their way up to Jerusalem for great feasts, which we know Jesus participated in from early boyhood through His last triumphal entry.[8]

In Jewish liturgy, Psalms 113–118 form the musical soundtrack of the Passover meal, psalms that Jesus and His disciples would have sung around the table each year, including at the last Passover meal, which we remember as the Last Supper (see Mark 14:26). Read these words from Psalm 116, bearing in mind the circumstances surrounding the night of Jesus' betrayal, and see which words or phrases stand out to you:

> What shall I return to the LORD
>    for all his goodness to me?
> I will lift up the cup of salvation
>    and call on the name of the LORD.
> I will fulfill my vows to the LORD
>    in the presence of all his people.
> Precious in the sight of the LORD
>    is the death of his faithful servants. (Psalm 116:12–16)

If you paused on "cup of salvation," "I will fulfill my vows," or "the death of his faithful servants," you're on the right track. These are the words Jesus would have sung just hours before His arrest, trial, and crucifixion. These very words were likely on Jesus' mind when He took the cup and said to His disciples: "This is my blood of the covenant, which is poured out for many for the forgiveness of sins" (Matthew 26:28).

---

Wednesday: Psalm 94–95:3; Thursday: Psalm 81; Friday: Psalm 93; Saturday: Psalm 92. "Psalms for Every Day of the Week," My Jewish Learning, accessed March 19, 2024, https://www.myjewishlearning.com/article/psalms-for-every-day-of-the-week/.

8. We know Jesus undertook these pilgrimages from early boyhood to His last triumphal entry that we celebrate on Palm Sunday (see Luke 2:41, John 2:13–16, John 4:45 for a smatter of sampling texts).

Also, listen to the echo of this psalm in Jesus' prayer in the garden of Gethsemane: "Father, if you are willing, take this cup from me; yet not my will, but yours be done" (Luke 22:42–44). Does this strike you as beautifully poetic as it does me? Have no doubt—Jesus' prayer life would have been infused with the Psalms, and He invites us to follow His example.

### Creative Ways to Pray the Word

As I mentioned, I grew up in a Christian tradition that valued spontaneous prayers more than scripted prayers. There was a general uneasiness about praying other people's words, so for years I only ever prayed in my own words.

I first learned to pray Scripture in Bible college, when I heard professors quoting and appropriating parts of Bible verses in their prayers. I resonated with the assurance that came from praying God's promises back to Him, and over time, it's become an effortless weaving of my words and God's words in prayer.

A few weeks into the 2020 COVID-19 lockdown, I found myself having a panic attack at the kitchen sink. I scrambled to the laundry room and slid to the floor, one thought pulsing through my brain: "I can't do this anymore." In response, God's Spirit brought to mind Psalm 46:1 to remind me of His presence even in my darkness: "God is our refuge and strength, a very present help in trouble." I prayed those words over and over, until His voice became louder than my anxious thoughts.

**If praying Scripture is new to you, you may want to start by picking a favorite psalm and slowly reading it out loud, verse by verse, pausing to personalize it to your own life. Allow the words of the psalm to serve as a springboard for your own thoughts in conversation with God.**

If the Psalms seem untenable for some reason, there are plenty of recorded prayers in the New Testament that serve as helpful guides; a few of my favorites are Ephesians 3:20–21, Philippians 2:5–11, and Jude 1:24–25.

God has brought to mind memorized Scripture to pray when I most needed it, whether for in my own desperation or when called upon to serve others—when I held my friend's hand in the ER as she went through a miscarriage, when I flew across the country to help another friend move out of an abusive relationship, and when I hold space for women to share their heavy stories after speaking at a conference.

There's power in praying the Word of God, not because God needs to be reminded, but because our own hearts need reassurance of what is ultimately true: God will keep His promises. So, we pray His Word to remember His faithfulness even on the darkest days.

## How Will You Delight in the Revelation of God?

I hope you've caught a vision for God's desire to reveal Himself to you as you open His Word every day. We follow His example by delighting in God's revelation, whether through leisurely feasts or quick snacks, or any other creative way. Once you embrace this adventure of weaving rhythms of God's Word into your day, you'll find Him restoring your joy in time.

Even though many church cultures value private Bible reading above other forms of Bible engagement, listening to the audio Bible while walking your dog isn't "less spiritual" than reading words on a page with a mug of coffee and a lit candle. Remember that Jesus heard, learned, memorized, spoke, and prayed the Word—so we can be like Jesus, delighting in the Word of God in lots of different ways.

As we create rhythms of being with Jesus by reading and meditating on the Word in our hands, He will reveal to us more and more of the Living Word—coming to life in our lives.

**Pick one of the creative ideas in this chapter or come up with your own. Then make a plan to weave your rhythm of the Word into the movements of your life.**

- How will you make this Rhythm of the Word small?

- What daily routines can you link to your word rhythm? "When I _____, I will _____."

- How can make your word rhythm fun and personal to you?

- How will you celebrate your growth each week? Month? Year?

God designed our brains to absorb and recall new information, so He knows how we can best form these rhythms of delighting in Him by dwelling in His Word. Ask Him to show you what daily tasks you can pair with your Bible habit, and ask Him to reveal Himself to you as you spend time with Jesus in the Word.

# CHAPTER 9

# Delighting in Communion with God: *Whisper*

G o, talk to the lady at the counter."

The whisper took my mom aback. She looked around the airport, taking in the empty chairs around her as tourists rushed out the revolving doors to get their first glimpse of the Acropolis and their first taste of baklava.

She wouldn't get to experience Athens because the lady at the counter was filling out her repatriation forms that very moment, forcefully sending her back to Romania, where the secret police would be waiting at the gate to arrest her and sentence her to a life in prison—all because she followed Jesus and invited others to follow Him too.

She rubbed her rotund belly, worry filling her heart. She would never see her baby girl if they sent her back; the communist prison guards would put her daughter in an orphanage. She would never again see her husband and toddler son, hiding this very moment, hoping she would make a way for their escape to Athens. She'd probably die in the frozen trenches of the Danube River, forced to work until her bones gave out.

"Go, talk to her," the whisper insisted. "Tell her your story."

With racing heart and shallow breaths, my mother obeyed the whisper.

"I don't even speak Greek," she whispered to the whisper, hauling herself to her swollen feet.

"Tell her your story," the whisper repeated. "I will give you the words."

She stepped up to the counter.

## Two-Way Prayer as Whispered Conversation with God

Stories like this one seem ripped from the pages of a novel, but all around the world, God's Spirit still moves His people in ways that seem fantastical to our twenty-first-century sensibilities.

We hear of dreams in the Middle East, as Jesus reveals Himself to Muslims who've never heard of Him.[1] We read stories of missionaries who asked God to meet their very specific needs and received a check with the exact amount in the mail later that week, often anonymously.[2]

---

1. See *Hearts of Fire: Eight Women in the Underground Church and Their Stories of Costly Faith* (Bartlesville, OK: Voice of the Martyrs, 2020), https://www.persecution.com/ heartsoffire.
2. For amazing stories of God answering prayers in miraculous and personal ways, two of my favorite books are George Müller's *Answers to Prayer* (Chicago: Moody Publishers, 2007), https://www.moody.edu/siteassets/landing-page-assets/launch-a-leader/ answers-to-prayer.pdf; and Silvia Tärniceriu's biography by Harvey Yoder, *God Knows My Size* (Berlin, OH: TGS International, 1999).

Yet our own lives seem oddly bereft of such miraculous encounters with the Lord.

Or are they?

How often have we felt the nudge to go talk to a stranger at a community function, but shrugged it off because it'd feel too weird? How often have we felt the prompting to stop and pray for someone who *randomly* popped into our minds, but we brushed it off as mere coincidence?

I've experienced both sides of these common scenarios: both when I ignored the whispered suggestions and when I listened to them. And over the years, I've learned to mostly discern when it's my own overactive imagination offering up suggestions, and when it's the voice of my heavenly Father. And *every time*, it's been worth the potential embarrassment of obedience.

I can't count the number of times I paused to pray for that random friend and sent them a quick text or voice message, just to hear back, "*How did you know?*" as they retell how my little message was confirmation of something they'd been praying about, or simply a reminder that God sees them and is listening to their cries. Honestly, it's unnerving sometimes. But more so, it's exhilarating in those moments to recognize that God's Spirit still speaks to His people today, prompting them to move, to speak, to act according to His will in the world. How can you be bored when every day holds the potential for an adventure with Jesus to unfold?

Can you imagine the shift in our lives—in our families and communities around the world—if we would learn to listen and follow Jesus' voice?

## The Good Shepherd Still Speaks

Scripture is full of encouragement to listen to God's voice as He directs His people. One of my favorites comes from John 10:

> I am the good shepherd; *I know my sheep and my sheep know me*—just as the Father knows me and I know the Father—and I lay down my life for the sheep. . . . *My sheep listen to my voice;* I know them, and they follow me. I give them eternal life, and they shall never perish; no one will snatch them out of my hand. My Father, who has given them to me, is greater than all; no one can snatch them out of my Father's hand. *I and the Father are one.* (John 10:14–15; 27–30)

Growing up in Romania, I got to see the verdant hills speckled with shepherds watching over their flocks and guiding their sheep with whistling, constant chatter, a guard dog, and their rod and staff. These shepherds didn't hide themselves from their flocks; they didn't make the sheep try to guess where they were supposed to go. Instead, these good shepherds stayed close to their flocks, reassuring them with their presence and their voices.

Building on this metaphor, Jesus claims that He is our Good Shepherd who desires to personally guide His sheep. When we slow down to listen to His voice and obey His whisper, we experience the joy of His personal presence, every moment of the day.

## As One Speaks to a Friend

I wonder, what image comes to mind when you hear the word *prayer*?

I used to think of prayer as a daily appointment that was both a privilege and an obligation. I thought it incredible that the Creator of the universe wanted to hear from me, but I also felt like He expected regular check-ins at a scheduled time that should last at least a half hour, probably due to well-meaning advice to "make a daily appointment with the Lord and keep it."

But what if prayer became less of a regular spiritual chore and more of a conversational friendship with God? What if God invites us to an ongoing exchange of whispers throughout our day—us whispering to Him and Him whispering right back to our hearts? What if our prayer lives reflected equitable amounts of both talking *and listening*?

I love this quote from Beth Moore:

> Prayer keeps us in constant communion with God, which is the goal of our entire believing lives. Without a doubt, prayerless lives are powerless lives and prayerful lives are powerful lives; but, believe it or not, the ultimate goal God has for us is not power but personal intimacy with Him.[3]

Prayer isn't just a spiritual discipline we should attempt because it makes us better Christians or grants us access to God's power. Prayer is the practice of communion with God, the kind of personal friendship that Moses experienced on Mount Sinai: "The LORD would speak to Moses face-to-face, as one speaks to a friend" (Exodus 33:11). This verse is the very first Bible verse I had my children memorize as toddlers, because I wanted them to know from a young age that our God longs for that kind of personal relationship with each of us.

---

3. Beth Moore, *Praying God's Word: Breaking Free from Spiritual Strongholds* (Nashville, TN: B&H Publishers, 2009), 6.

# Radiating with Joy

The Bible tells us that as wonderful as Moses' friendship with God was, we get something better:

> Therefore, since we have such a hope, we are very bold. We are not like Moses, who would put a veil over his face to prevent the Israelites from seeing the end of what was passing away. . . . And we all, who with unveiled faces contemplate the Lord's glory, are being transformed into his image with ever-increasing glory, which comes from the Lord, who is the Spirit. (2 Corinthians 3:12–13, 18)

Did you catch that? There is *so much richness* in those verses that I encourage you to pull out your Bible and read the verses in their proper context. Underline, highlight, and mark the words that stand out to you. And spend some time right now responding to the God who would invite you into such close proximity to Himself. Go ahead . . . I'll wait.

Are you back? Good. Did you notice how Paul compares followers of Jesus to Moses? Whatever Moses had with God on Mount Sinai, *we have something better.* Whoa.

Moses' mediation of the old covenant was glorious, but ultimately fading and ineffective. But Jesus' mediation of the new covenant is glorious, eternal, and transformative. Because of Jesus, our experience of God's presence doesn't have to fade over time . . . we get continual, ongoing, nonstop access to the God who created us for delight. And, in fact, the radiance of God's presence doesn't fade . . . we get to go "from glory to glory" as He transforms us more and more like Jesus.[4]

---

4. Jesus says this Himself in John 17:22: "I have given them the glory you gave me."

And did you pick up on the mirror imagery in this passage? Paul further develops this idea in 1 Corinthians 13:12: "Now we see but a dim reflection as in a mirror; then we shall see face to face." Just like Moses, face-to-face. Can you imagine what a glorious day that will be—when we turn from the dim mirror to finally behold the glory of God face-to-face? "Now I know in part; then I shall know fully, even as I am fully known."

What would change in our lives if we actually believed that? If we actually approached God to speak with Him boldly, confidently, as we would with a friend? What if we spoke with Him throughout our day, whispering to Him as we went about our day? What if we set aside time each day to gaze so intently on His glory that we actually started glowing from being with Him?

In those places in our lives where we feel burdened, broken, or burned-out, God invites us into this rhythm of ongoing communion with Him. And as we commune with God, conversing with Him throughout our day, He will restore our joy. For as the psalmist says: "Those who look to him are radiant with joy; their faces will never be ashamed" (Psalm 34:5 CSB).

## A Reputation of Guiding His People

Jesus' claim to personally guide His flock would have resonated with His first-century listeners. After all, it's exactly what God had done for His people throughout their desert wanderings—albeit in a pillar of cloud by day and a pillar of fire by night (see Exodus 13:21). And throughout the Hebrew Scriptures, God used the imagery of shepherd and sheep to describe His relationship with His people. Jesus' first-century listeners would have recognized His appropriation of this metaphor from the Old Testament prophecies promising just such a Messiah.

Look how David described the Lord as a shepherd present with His flock as He guides them in the path of life:

> He makes me lie down in green pastures,
> he leads me beside quiet waters,
>   he refreshes my soul.
> *He guides me along the right paths*
>   for his name's sake. (Psalm 23:2–3)

And in the book of Isaiah, God used this same imagery to describe how the Messiah would lead His people:

> See, the Sovereign LORD comes with power . . .
> *He tends his flock like a shepherd*:
>   He gathers the lambs in his arms
> and carries them close to his heart;
>   he gently leads those that have young. (Isaiah 40:10–11)

In another Isaiah passage that doesn't directly state the shepherd imagery, God paints a vivid picture of how involved the Messiah will be guiding His people in the way they should go: "Your Teacher will not hide any longer. Your eyes will see your Teacher, and whenever you turn to the right or to the left, *your ears will hear this command behind you: 'This is the way. Walk in it'"* (Isaiah 30:20–21 CSB).

*This is the way. Walk in it.*

Don't you wish sometimes that God spoke so clearly to your heart? A friend and I often joke that we wish God would send us a postcard in the mail or a plane in the sky to spell out exactly what is the next right step in our motherhood, our marriages, or our ministries. We plead, "Just tell us, God, and I'll do it."

It's in those moments when God's voice is difficult to discern that it's time for honest self-reflection: Are we really listening?

# "Unplugging" Our Ears to Hear

The problem is not that God doesn't speak to us. More likely, the problem is that *we* don't stop to listen to His voice.

If you've ever felt that tension of wanting to talk to God and hear His voice but not being able to hear yourself think (let alone hear God speak!), please know that you're not alone. I've experienced this very frustrating reality, as have millions of Jesus followers around the world. A 2019 Crossway survey found that only 2 percent of Christians are *very satisfied* with their prayer lives, and 57 percent would say that the biggest obstacle to prayer is distraction, followed by indifference (15 percent), busyness (15 percent), and a loss for words (13 percent).[5]

> When we're too busy to pray, we're too busy to see God moving in our lives.

Not everyone who is exposed to God's Word will learn to discern His voice. Like the teachers of the Law in Jesus' time who were "ever hearing but never understanding" and "ever seeing but never perceiving" (see Matthew 13:12–17), so we too can be exposed to both Scripture and the Spirit's promptings but fail to discern His voice in our lives.

When we're too busy to pray, we're too busy to see God moving in our lives. Of course, we know that prayer is important, and we hope to someday become "better" at praying, but frankly there's too much going on right now for us to get serious about learning to pray. And anyway, prayer often feels like a one-way conversation—us telling God all about our lives and problems—so how could prayer help us hear God's voice?

5. "Infographic: How Is Your Prayer Life?," Crossway, November 2, 2019, https://www.crossway.org/articles/infographic-how-is-your-prayer-life/.

Maybe you, like me, have tried setting aside ten minutes to pray, only to get distracted within forty-five seconds. And these distractions come not just outside of us (notifications on our phones, family members walking through the house, the neighbor trimming his hedges—*this very minute, of all times!*), but also by the incessant noise inside our heads too.

It seems like as soon as I sit down to pray, I remember the meat that needs to be pulled out of the freezer for dinner, the friend whose birthday is coming up and I still need to buy a gift for, or the bill that's sitting on the counter and needs to be paid. It feels like the universe is conspiring against us as soon as we pause to pray! These mental and external distractions can become a sort of spiritual ear plug that muffles the whisper of God's "still, small voice" in our modern world and in our multitasking hearts.[6]

These are all valid reasons we struggle to pray, but there's one compelling reason to pray anyway: Jesus stands ready to help us.

## How Jesus Prays for Us

My prayer life radically changed the moment I realized that Jesus is actually praying for me.

I mean, I knew that He prayed for all His followers in the garden of Gethsemane on the night He was betrayed, and it's a beautiful prayer, one I'm deeply grateful for. But I didn't realize that Jesus continues to pray for me and for you, even this very moment you're reading this.

One afternoon, I was reading a passage in Isaiah and followed the footnoted verses that took me to Hebrews 7:25. It wasn't the first time I'd read this verse, but as we discussed in the previous chapter, when we read Scripture in dependence on God's Spirit

---

6. See 1 Kings 19:12–13.

and ask Him to open our eyes to see new wonders in His Word, He actually does it. And that day, God opened my eyes to understand a bit more of the wonder of Jesus' intercessory ministry for us.

Hebrews 7:25 reads: "Therefore, he is able to save completely those who come to God through him, *since he always lives to intercede for them*" (CSB). This word, "intercede" is not one we use often outside of religious contexts, but it means to make a petition, to plead with a person, often for the purpose of asking favor, or to pray on behalf of another.[7]

This intercession is not just on the issue of salvation, because the same word is used of Jesus' ongoing ministry of prayer through His Spirit:

> And he who searches our hearts knows the mind of the Spirit, because *he intercedes for the saints* according to the will of God. (Romans 8:27 CSB)

> Christ Jesus is the one who died, but even more, has been raised; he also is at the right hand of God *and intercedes for us*. (Romans 8:34 CSB)

I hope you're beginning to see this picture of Jesus, standing at the right hand of God, praying for you. Not just when you have the words to pray, but even when you struggle to pray, even when you get distracted in your prayers, even when you feel like your prayers are hitting the ceiling—especially then.

Because Jesus is fully God and fully human, He is our High Priest who intimately knows all our weaknesses while being perfect in every way; so He knows how best to intercede for us:

---

7. "Blue Letter Bible Lexicon - G1793, *entygchanō*," Blue Letter Bible, https://www .blueletterbible.org/lexicon/g1793/kjv/tr/0-1/.

> Therefore, since we have a great high priest who has passed
> through the heavens—Jesus the Son of God—let us hold fast
> to our confession. For we do not have a high priest who is
> unable to sympathize with our weaknesses, but one who has
> been tempted in every way as we are, yet without sin. There-
> fore, let us approach the throne of grace with boldness, so
> that we may receive mercy and find grace to help us in time of
> need. (Hebrews 4:14–16 CSB)

Thank God that He provided for us not just an opportunity to pray, but also a perfect Mediator who prays for us in our weaknesses. As our High Priest, Jesus opens the way to God the Father, but He also represents God to us. He is our go-between. We can come boldly to His throne to receive all we need, knowing that even when we pray imperfectly, our perfect High Priest carries our prayers to His Father and adds His prayers to our own.

Pause to ponder that for a moment: If you could overhear Jesus praying for you in the other room, what would He be praying for you?

What a powerful picture this is. We're not begging God to do something He doesn't want, and we're not imposing on Jesus with our needs like whiny children, but rather we're joining Him in what He's already doing: praying for us.

And better yet—Jesus sent His own Spirit, our Comforter, who prays with groanings when we can't. Even when we don't know what to pray, we can simply come to Jesus, and be with Him, and He'll do the praying.

This doesn't mean we ignore prayer and go about our day oblivious to Jesus' intercession on our behalf. On the contrary, it means learning to sit with God in silence sometimes. It means becoming aware of God's loving presence even while we're wail-ing, even while we're sobbing, even while we're angry, even when we have no words. Instead of trying to escape it by scrolling social media or numbing ourselves with food or drink, we sit with Jesus in the discomfort, leaning into Him, letting Him hold us up when we can't hold ourselves.

Jesus stands willing to help, if only we would come to Him.

Our prayers don't have to be impressive. They don't have to be long. They don't have to quote large swaths of Scripture. They simply need to be from the heart. And they do have to happen. Even if it's just a whispered "Jesus!" in the middle of a crisis, our hearts learn to cry out to Him.

As we learn to sit with Jesus as He prays for us through His Spirit, we'll begin to hear His still, small voice in the quiet. And the more often we hear His voice in the quiet, the more we learn to recognize His voice in the noise. Just as I can pick up the timbre of my husband's laugh or storytelling across a crowded room, we'll learn to discern the whisper of our Good Shepherd in the noisiness of daily life.

## The God Who Still Speaks Today

Going back to the opening story of this chapter that day in the Athens airport . . .

My mother trusted the whisper even though she didn't trust the lady at the counter.

She showed the woman a black-and-white photo of the husband and child she'd left behind, and in her broken English and French pieced together why she was fleeing communist Romania and what would await her if she were sent back. A life of forced labor, simply because she followed Jesus and invited others to follow Him too.

And that December day in 1987, a miracle happened in a small cubicle in the airport in Athens, Greece. The hard heart of this airline employee softened as she leaned in. "Tell me more," she said.

Twenty-one years after my mother's miraculous deliverance, she took me back to Athens to meet that same woman—Fanny— whose name I carry as my middle name, to walk the halls of the crisis pregnancy center that housed my mother in the weeks leading up to her labor and delivery, to sit in the sacred space where a scared twenty-one-year-old pregnant girl listened to a still, small voice.

The three of us sat around Fanny's dining room table, enjoying an authentic Greek meal.

"I wasn't even supposed to be there," Fanny told me as she dished out homemade eggplant *papoutsakia* at her dining room table. "My shift had ended an hour before, so imagine how annoyed I was when my supervisor gave me extra paperwork to extradite this pregnant foreigner to her homeland."

"But God kept you there," my mom said, filling up the water glasses. "For me. For us."

Fanny laughed as she put her arm around my mother. "No one else in that airport knew the people I knew and could call in the favors that I called. And that—" she said, locking eyes with me, a stranger and yet her goddaughter, "is how your mother came to live here for a year." I stopped setting the table, mesmerized by her piercing gaze. "That is how *you* were born here."

Sitting at that table with Fanny and my mother, I felt overwhelmed by the power and tender love of God. The One who would hear the cries of a lonely and unknown girl far from home. The One who would soften a tired and overworked airline employee's heart to take time to listen to a story. The One who would whisper into the chaos of an international airport to save a life.

This is our God. The One who delights in you and longs for you to hear His tender whispers guiding you in the way you should go.

How do we slow down the hustle, quiet the inner chatter, and tame the busyness to actually hear God's still, small voice speaking to us today?

Let's look at the example of Jesus.

# CHAPTER 10

# Practicing Jesus' Rhythm of Whisper

You might be wondering, "Why use the word 'whisper' to describe prayer?"

Well, aside from my ridiculous love for alliteration, I've always been fascinated by the biblical instruction to "pray without ceasing" (see 1 Thessalonians 5:17). Too many preachers have written off this verse as being unrealistic. "It doesn't really mean to pray all the time," they reason. "After all, you can't pray while you're presenting quarterly gains in a board meeting or having a conversation with a friend."

But what if that verse means exactly what it says?

What if it's actually possible to be in communion and conversation with God *all the time*? The apostle Paul seems to have thought it perfectly reasonable to have a rich internal dialog with the Spirit of God indwelling us, so maybe it's our understanding of prayer that needs to change. We can learn to become so attuned to God's still, small voice that we hear His whisper interrupt our thoughts even while we're going about our day.

*We can learn to become so attuned to God's still, small voice that we hear His whisper interrupt our thoughts even while we're going about our day.*

As we learned in the previous chapter, God wants to communicate with us— and us to communicate with Him— throughout our day, not just in structured times of prayer (though we'll talk about both in this chapter). There's an assumption that we'd go about our days in a quiet state of expectancy, listening for God's still, small voice to speak to us through His Spirit.

But as I was discussing this metaphor of prayer as a whisper with my friends, I realized that my prayer life isn't always accurately defined as a whisper. Sometimes prayer means wondering aloud: "God, what are You doing? Where are You in this? God, what do You want me to do next?"

Sometimes we're wailing in prayer (quite loudly I might add). Scripture supports this manner of prayer, even claiming that part of our role as God's holy priests in the world is to lament that which is broken and hurting (see Romans 8:18–30). Over the past few years, the conflict and human tragedies that have filled the headlines have caused more than one prayer time of wailing, and I'm comforted that the Psalms are filled with lament too.

Please don't feel like your prayers have to be in a librarian-approved "inside voice" just because of the title of this chapter. We'll use the metaphor of whisper to remind our souls to be in continual conversation with God throughout the day, but feel free to replace the word "whisper" with whatever other metaphor best fits this rhythm of delight in your life.

God Himself speaks to us in different tones too. As C. S. Lewis wrote, "We can ignore even pleasure. But pain insists upon being attended to. *God whispers to us in our pleasures,* speaks in our conscience, but shouts in our pains: it is his megaphone to rouse a deaf world."[1]

I don't know about you, but I don't want God to have to shout at me in my pain in order to get my attention. Don't get me wrong—He absolutely has used pain in my life to rouse me. In my tiring seasons of burnout and brokenness, I sometimes wondered whether God had gone silent or if my own ears were somehow plugged. Looking back in those moments where I felt alone and abandoned, I can now recognize the markers of my Good Shepherd carrying me close to His heart, so that even though I didn't see or hear Him, He'd never been closer.

Pain has a way of stripping away the fluff, quieting the noise, and eventually bringing us face-to-face with our Creator. Perhaps you've experienced the same in your life too. God uses pain to get our attention. But I don't want pain to be the only way I hear God's voice; I don't want Him to have to shout before I pause to listen.

I want to learn to hear God's whisper even in the good times, in the noisy spaces, and in uncertain places.

## Learning to Discern God's Still, Small Voice

Maybe you've reached this point and you're wondering, "How do I know if it's God's voice or if it's my own subconscious talking?"

---

1. C. S. Lewis, *The Problem of Pain* (South Korea: HarperOne, 2001), Kindle, 59. Emphasis added.

That's a legitimate question, and while Scripture does not give us a three-step process to discern God's voice, there are some wise principles we can put into practice to grow our discernment when it comes to listening to God's voice.

About 30 to 50 percent of people experience ongoing internal monologues, and the rest of us still face an internal soundtrack that's shaped by the media we consume, the company we keep, and the language we grew up with.[2] Not every thought that pops into our minds comes from God, which is why Scripture compels us to "be transformed by the renewing of our minds" (see Romans 12:1–2). We're to "take every thought captive to make it obedient to Christ" (see 2 Corinthians 10:5). And as we partner with God's Spirit in this work, we gradually change to "have the mind of Christ"—that is, to think the thoughts of God after Him (see 1 Corinthians 2:16). Here are some principles to consider:

## Listen to How His Voice Sounds in Scripture

We have God's Word preserved for us in the pages of our Bibles, so we know how He speaks and what is in keeping with His character based on what He's already revealed in the pages of Scripture. Most often, when I sense God speaking to me, it's through snippets of Bible verses that He brings to mind: He's teaching me to walk in His commands. As we learn what the voice of our Good Shepherd sounds like in Scripture, we can compare what we "hear" to what's already been spoken in Scripture. God will never contradict Himself (more on the importance of this truth below).

2. Kyle D. Killian, "How Inner Monologues Work, and Who Has Them," *Psychology Today*, April 25, 2023, https://www.psychologytoday.com/us/blog/intersections/202304/inner-monologues-what-are-they-and-whos-having-them.

## Learn His Voice in the Quiet

Because I've been friends with my husband for over twenty years, I can pick out the timbre of his voice and lilt of his laugh even in a crowded room. We're so attuned to one another after years of companionable friendship that I can pick up on subtle shifts in his voice, whether anxiety, amusement, or anger, even when these subtleties might be lost on acquaintances. That intimate knowledge has grown and deepened over years. So too with our Good Shepherd's voice, the more we listen to Him in the quiet of our secret place with Him, the more attuned we'll become to His voice in the chaos of everyday life.

## Test the Whispers Against His Word

Whenever you wonder if a thought comes from God, from yourself, or from the enemy, search the Scriptures to see if it aligns with God's own Word. We see Jesus doing this very thing when Satan tempted Him in the wilderness. Three times, Jesus responded, "It is written . . ." as He quoted God's truth to counteract Satan's lies. Ask a friend to help you if you're unfamiliar with the Bible. The more we get into God's Word and God's Word gets into our hearts, the more quickly and easily we'll distinguish between Satan's lies and God's truth. We'll also learn to discern between the accuser's slanderous condemnation that drives us away from God and the Spirit's conviction that drives us closer to God. And consider too whether this thought makes much of God or much of ourselves. God's whisper is less like a neon sign flashing brightly to fame and success and more like a flickering candle showing us the next right step in humble dependence on His Spirit.

Over the years, I've made a practice of pausing in the middle of my structured times of prayer to seek God's stillness, to practice listening to His voice. I often echo Samuel's prayer when he thought he heard a voice: "Speak, Lord, for your servant is listening" (see 1 Samuel 3:7–11). And then I practice listening. I might write in my journal the thoughts that come to mind and then test them against Scripture or talk to a trusted friend about what I heard. Sometimes, I don't hear anything at all, in which case I practice amicable silence, pondering God's great love for me, simply content to gaze upon the One whom my soul loves. And sometimes I echo the prayer my friend Judy prays whenever we start a work meeting, "Lord, may Your voice be the loudest in this room."

Now it's time to turn our attention to the practice of prayer as Whisper, looking first at the life of Jesus.

## Jesus' Rhythm of Prayer as Two-Way Conversation with God

Many of us have heard the dictum that we should rise before dawn to spend our first hour in prayer because Jesus woke up early to go off by Himself and pray. Preachers cite those few verses so often, you'd think that's the only way that Jesus prayed (and by implication, the "best" way for us to pray). But as we survey the Gospels, we see that Jesus prayed in lots of different ways, and that gives us the freedom to embrace creativity as we learn to pray like Jesus.[3] Let's take a look at some of the ways that Jesus prayed.

### Jesus Prayed All Day Long

While He did sometimes wake up early in the morning to pray by Himself (see Mark 1:35), a careful reading of Scripture reveals that

---

3. Many of these examples of Jesus' model of prayer were inspired by Robert Velarde's article "Learning from the Prayer Life of Jesus," Focus on the Family, January 1, 2008, https://www.focusonthefamily.com/faith/learning-from-the-prayer-life-of-jesus/.

Jesus prayed all day, not just in the morning. Morning prayers are not "better" than evening prayers or sit-in-the-carpool-line prayers.

Actually, Jewish tradition required men to pray three times a day—morning, afternoon, and evening—corresponding to the three daily sacrifices that were offered in the temple in Jerusalem.[4] As a faithful Jew, Jesus would have likely observed this practice, as did His followers in Jerusalem (see Acts 3:1 and 10:9).

Jesus prayed throughout the day, whenever He had need, even at times staying up all night (see Luke 6:12). The point here is not to develop a rigorous schedule in hopes of imitating Jesus, but rather to develop the rhythm of talking with God all day long— not just at a legalistically set time of day. It's in this way that we'll learn to "pray without ceasing" (see 1 Thessalonians 5:17).

## Jesus Prayed Alone and with Others, Inside and Outside

We live in such an individualistic society that praying out loud with others might cause some of us to break out in hives. But when we look to the life of Jesus, we see that He prayed both alone—often withdrawing to "lonely places" for focused time in prayer (see Luke 5:16)—and with others, like when He took Peter, James, and John with Him up a mountainside to pray together (see Luke 9:28). And on the hardest night of His life, Jesus turned to these same three friends and asked them to pray and watch with Him (see Matthew 26:36–46).

The New Testament also records more than ten times when Jesus participated in services at the local synagogue, which is a

---

4. Though not found in the Torah, this tradition of praying three times a day facing the temple mount was so defining for a faithful Jew that Daniel's enemies could count on his regular prayers even while he was in exile (see Daniel 6:10–11).

community's meeting house for prayer and study of the Torah. By implication, this means Jesus prayed both inside as well as outside (see Luke 6:12), which gives us freedom to do the same.

### Jesus Prayed Short and Long Prayers

We also see variety in the length of Jesus' prayers, as He both "spent the night praying to God" (see Luke 6:12) and prayed short prayers too, like at Lazarus' tomb and when He multiplied the bread and fish for the multitude. In this, Jesus models prayer as long conversations with His heavenly Father as well as short "whispers" throughout the day.

### Jesus Prayed for Himself and for Others

As we've already seen, Jesus spent long hours in conversation with His heavenly Father, in solitude, and likely combining times of silence with times of worship. We can read His prayer in John 17 as an example of both honest wrestling with the hard thing He was facing the night of His betrayal, as well as an example of complete surrender to His Father's will. In this, Jesus picks up the tradition of the Psalms as a prayer book, a glimpse into honest prayers about hard emotions.

But Jesus also prayed for others, as when He blessed the children who came to Him (Matthew 19:13 and John 17:9), and when He interceded for His disciples, especially Peter: "Simon, Simon, Satan has asked to sift all of you as wheat. But I have prayed for you, Simon, that your faith may not fail" (Luke 22:31–32).

Following in Jesus' footsteps, we can learn to be honest with God about the hard emotions and tricky situations we find ourselves in, holding nothing back from Him in prayerful conversation. And we can also grow in the ministry of intercessory prayer, praying on others' behalf with boldness and confidence.

## Jesus Prayed Spontaneous Prayers and Written Prayers

In the middle of a conversation with people who both despised Him and desired Him, Jesus (seemingly randomly) breaks out in a public prayer that may seem odd to most of us (it's definitely not listed in the category of how to win friends and influence people), but it reveals the spontaneous and heartfelt kinds of conversations—perhaps even a whispered conversation—that Jesus had with His Father: "I thank You, that You've hidden these things . . ."

And as we saw at length in the previous rhythm (chapter 8), Jesus prayed the written Psalms in both His personal prayers and in corporate worship. We have a few recorded prayers, most notably Matthew 6 and John 17, so we can look at the language Jesus uses and see the familiarity and also deference that He uses in these two examples.

## Freedom to Pray with Boldness, Confidence, and Creativity

As we can see from Jesus' example, *there is no one "right" way to pray*, as long as we are coming with sincere hearts to our heavenly Father through Jesus Christ. If you're bringing your everything to Jesus, *you're doing it right*, because God's own Spirit will guide you into learning how to pray.

Jesus' disciples recognized that He prayed differently than the other religious leaders of His day, which is why they asked Him to teach them how to pray (see Luke 11:1). This posture of humble learning is actually a great place to start: ask Jesus to help you. Ask Him to teach you, to personally guide you deeper into prayer. This prayer honors Him, and He always answers it!

I can remember writing that very prayer in my journal as a thirteen-year-old: "Teach me how to pray, Lord, like You taught your disciples." I earnestly desired to grow in my boldness and confidence in conversation with God, and He graciously answered my prayer by personally guiding me through the landscape of deeper conversation with Him. And over the years, He's given me the freedom to pray in lots of different ways, embracing creativity and delight as I stay attuned to His whisper and respond to Him throughout my day.

### Learning to Pray Together

Over the years, I've learned so much by praying with others. My parents were the first who taught me how to pray, but God used others too: my friend Carmen taught me the sweetness of persistent prayer; my friend Jennifer taught me the power of Scripture prayer; my friend Niki taught me the thrill of prophetic prayer.

Because Jesus intercedes for us as our High Priest, we are all on equal footing when we pray together. I love how Megan Hill expresses this:

> A company of praying people is a company of people equally dependent on God. But we also come to prayer with equally good help. The most eloquent spiritual giant and the most timid new believer can pray boldly together because Jesus prays for them both.[5]

Instead of being intimidated by others' prayer lives, we can learn from them and allow their fervor to stir up our own. When

---

5. Megan Hill, *Praying Together: The Priority and Privilege of Prayer in Our Homes, Communities, and Churches* (Wheaton, IL: Crossway, 2016), 59.

my first daughter was a newborn, my husband and I had just joined a new church, and an acquaintance invited me to join a prayer and worship gathering in her home. I was nervous about going, since I didn't know anyone, but a hunger for fellowship with other Jesus-loving women drove me to overcome my social anxiety and show up anyway.

*It's just once,* I reasoned as I parked my car and walked to her front door. *I don't have to come back if it's weird.* Small talk is hard for me; it was hard that evening, and it's still hard today. But once we began singing a few a cappella songs, I realized this gathering wasn't about me; it was about coming together to honor Jesus. And then we started praying, taking turns as one woman led us through prayers of adoration, confession, thanksgiving, and intercession. Two hours later, I couldn't believe how quickly the time had gone by.

I went back the next month, and the month after that, and after that. We gathered for three years, sometimes alternating homes, sometimes prayer-walking around schools, sometimes meeting at our church. I grew so much in my desire to pray, and my confidence in praying out loud, and my boldness to ask our heavenly Father big things, because I prayed with these sweet women. It's there I realized that "we learn to pray not by reading a book or sitting in a lecture, but by actually praying together."[6]

Have you ever experienced the power of praying together? Ask God's Spirit to bring to mind a few friends or neighbors who may want to join you in prayer. You'll find plenty of resources online to guide you in how to start a prayer group, and you can even use an audio prayer guide like my free *Prayers of REST* podcast to lead

6. I write more about the power of praying together in my book *Prayers of REST: Daily Prompts to Slow Down and Hear God's Voice* (Chicago: Moody Publishers, 2022), 12.

your group if you don't feel comfortable at first.[7] Remember, the point is not to impress anyone with our prayers, but to join arms as we approach God's throne of grace with confidence together. He is the One we're praying to, after all.

## Short Breath Prayers

One way I've found helpful to remain aware of God's presence and listening to His whisper throughout my day is to practice short breath prayers at regular intervals throughout the day.

Christians have practiced breath prayers for hundreds of years, simply synchronizing a short Scripture prayer to each breath in a way that calms both mind and body. I often use the Psalms as inspiration, but you can use any promise from Scripture, dividing the first part of the verse for my slow, deep inhale, and then praying the second half of the verse during my slow, deep exhale.[8] Here are a few examples:

> Inhale: *God is our refuge and strength*
> Exhale: *A very present help in time of trouble* (see Psalm 46:1)

Or . . .

> Inhale: *Nothing can separate me*
> Exhale: *From Your love* (see Romans 8:38–39)

Or . . .

7. Learn more and download a leaders' guide for prayer groups at www.prayersof rest.com.
8. One resource I've appreciated on this topic is Jennifer Tucker's beautifully illustrated book, *Breath as Prayer: Calm Your Anxiety, Focus Your Mind, and Renew Your Soul* (Nashville: Thomas Nelson, 2022).

Inhale: *He who began a good work in me*
Exhale: *Will be faithful to complete it* (see Philippians 1:6)

Combining deep breathing with meditative prayer, while not explicitly seen in Scripture, aligns with the many calls to find our rest in God's loving presence. It's one of the many ways we can quiet our souls with Him:

Truly my soul finds rest in God;
my salvation comes from him. . . .
Yes, my soul, find rest in God;
my hope comes from him. (Psalm 62:1, 5)

I've tried to create a rhythm of practicing breath prayers while washing my hands, or while filling my glass with water. By connecting this rhythm to something I regularly do throughout my day, I'm reminded to slow down and listen for God's whisper all day long.

## Longer Times of Prayer as REST

During the 2020 lockdown, I gathered with a group of women online to pray every morning for a half hour for months. I'd read a short passage, and then we'd pray that Scripture using the REST acronym I'll explain next. Those half hours of prayer were what kept us grounded during a time of global upheaval, and we experienced the peace of God guarding our hearts and minds in miraculous ways.[9] Here's how I and my fellow prayer partners have learned to rest in prayer:

---

9. Over time, those gatherings became a prayer podcast, with thousands of people around the world praying with us week after week, and eventually a book, *Prayers of REST: Daily Prompts to Slow Down and Hear God's Voice* (Chicago: Moody Publishers, 2022).

### RECITE God's goodness

We begin by praising God for who He is and what He has done in our lives. If you're praying through a Bible passage, look for attributes of God that can lead you in worship. Look for ways where God has demonstrated that attribute in your life, and thank Him for specific ways He has revealed His goodness to you.

### EXPRESS your neediness

As we gaze on the beauty of God's character, we become more aware of our own sinfulness and desperate need for God. Take time to confess your sins and ask God for forgiveness and His Spirit's growth in this area of your life. If you're praying through a passage, identify specific failures or needs that the text might highlight, confident that it is God's pleasure to give you His kingdom.[10]

### SEEK His stillness

Prayer isn't just about talking; it's about learning to listen. After expressing our needs, we rejoice in God's promise to forgive us, cleanse us, and restore to us the joy of our salvation. Take time to be still before the Lord, becoming aware of His loving presence surrounding you and filling you through His Spirit. Quiet your heart and listen as He speaks to you in His still, small voice.

### TRUST His faithfulness

We find rest for our souls by reminding ourselves how God has been faithful to His promises throughout history and throughout our lives. We entrust our heavy burdens to His loving care, confident that He will be faithful to complete the good work He

10. See Luke 12:32.

has started in us and through us, as He will in the world too. You might want to end your prayer by declaring to Him and to yourself: God, I trust You.

The acronym itself, REST, reminds us that God invites us to cease striving, to stop worrying, to pause our hustling, and to rest in Him. These longer times of prayer will help ingrain the acronym in your memory, becoming an easy-to-retrieve mnemonic device that becomes your lifeline when anxiety takes your breath away and worry keeps you up at night. You'll learn to pray the REST way whether for thirty minutes or thirty seconds, learning to become aware of God's loving presence around you and empowering you to rest in Him.

## Other Creative Ideas for Whisper as a Rhythm of Delight

Here are a few other creative ways to pray, all of which have found their way into my daily rhythm of prayer at one point or another over the past thirty years:

> **Read written prayers as a springboard to your own spontaneous prayers.** Some of the prayer collections I've enjoyed over the years include the Puritan *Valley of Vision*, the more contemporary *Every Moment Holy*, and my own *Prayers of REST*.

> **Listen to a guided prayer podcast when you're commuting** to school or work and pray along. I've listened to several prayer podcasts before starting the *Prayers of REST* podcast in 2020. You can find a few of my favorites at www.delightinginjesus.com/book-resources.

**Create your own collection of Scripture prayer cards.**
My friend Jennifer inspired me with her prayer cards:
simple handwritten index cards featuring a promise from
God's Word and the family member or life situation she
was praying that for. You can see some of my collections at
www.delightinginjesus.com/book-resources.

**Start a legacy prayer Bible.** My mom did this before it was
trendy on Instagram, but it's never too late to join. Simply
jot short Scripture-inspired prayers in the margins of a
journaling Bible, adding the date for each prayer. You can
also personalize a prayer Bible for each child or grandchild
to give as a legacy and a blessing. What a special gift.

**Practice prayer journaling a few times a week.** If you,
like me, struggle to be consistent journaling every day, try
to write just a one-sentence prayer, creating a touch point
with God for each day. Or set a fifteen-minute timer and
write out your honest conversation with God.

**Try a 28-day Whisper challenge.** If you struggle to stay
focused in private prayer, try whispering your prayers,
picturing Jesus sitting in the chair across from you.

**Take a prayer walk around your neighborhood.** If you're
already walking your dog or in the habit of daily walks,
link your prayer habit to what you're already doing. Pray
for your neighbors as you pass their houses; pray for local
authorities, for emergency personnel, for schools and their
leadership.

**Create prayer prompts for every day of the week.** I keep all my prayer requests in a journal that's divided by days of the week:

- Monday: our world, nation, community, and local church
- Tuesday: my husband, children, and extended family
- Wednesday: sweet friends and those who don't yet know Jesus
- Thursday: personal needs, challenges, fears, and dreams
- Friday: ministry projects, like speaking, writing, and podcasting
- Weekend: reflect on the week and write down God's answers to prayer[11]

## How Will You Delight in Communion with God?

Are you excited yet? Simply reading through that list of creative ideas, I want to go back and start some of them again. To be clear, I don't practice all these prayer habits all the time; they come and go with seasons. Certain methods of prayer fit better with certain times of the year. The point here is not to rigorously repeat the same thing every day, but to create a rhythm of communion with God that flows with our days.

**As you think about your current season of life, which of the**

---

11. I've used a regular spiral notebook for this topical prayer journal for years, but now there are many lovely options to choose from. You can watch a video of how I format my prayer journal, as well as my current favorite products at www.delightinginjesus .com/book-resources.

ideas above might you try to add to the rhythm of your day?
What might it look like to whisper with God throughout your
day, keeping in conversation with Him from morning to night?

- How can you start your Rhythm of Whisper small?

- What daily routines can you link to your whisper rhythm?
  "When I _____, I will _____."

- How can you make your whisper enjoyable and personal to
  you?

- How will you celebrate your growth each week? Month? Year?

Staying in conversation with God throughout our day not only
reminds us of His presence with us, but it also opens our eyes to
see His hand at work in the world and in our own lives, which is
where we turn next.

# CHAPTER 11

# Delighting in the Gifts of God: *Wonder*

We had no running water. For years.

When I was seven years old, my family moved to Romania as missionaries to the Roma. We lived in a little village an hour away from the nearest city in a tiny cabin that lacked running water or indoor plumbing for the first four years.

I learned how to lower a wooden bucket into a stone-hewn well and draw the bucket full of water back up again, then haul it up the hill to our cabin (though, thankfully, that was usually my older brother's job). My job was to wash our dishes by heating water on a portable stovetop, and then carefully scrubbing and rinsing the dishes in alternate bowls of precious water. Showers became a weekly luxury, a convenience enjoyed on our trips to the big city.

But what our tiny house lacked in comfort, it made up for in scenery.

Our log cabin sat atop a hill, offering an unobstructed view of the terra-cotta roofs in front of us, the untamed forest behind us, and the Carpathian Mountains off into the eastern distance. Just beyond the smattering of plastered houses lay verdant fields of grain, corn, and barley, as far as the eye could see.

But my favorite spot was the wide window in my matchbox bedroom. Facing west, it offered the very best view of God's artistic handiwork each evening, when the sun setting on the horizon painted a variegated sky brilliant shades of ochre, rose, violet, azure, and gold.

I'd sit at my bedroom window, mesmerized by the shifting hues that created a new scene every few minutes. *God is doing this*, I'd marvel. *And every evening, I get to watch Him do it.* It felt like a gift, this special moment shared just between the two of us, despite being displayed for the whole world to see.

My awe of God's artistry didn't dim when I learned the scientific explanation for colorful sunsets: light rays hitting air particles in the atmosphere and changing wavelengths to create a dazzling display of color. If anything, the science only increased my wonder at the skies set ablaze.

Years later, when I'd sit in my college British Literature class reading Gerard Manley Hopkins for the first time, it's these blazing sunsets from my bedroom window that I'd picture:

> The world is charged with the grandeur of God.
>     It will flame out, like shining from shook foil;
> It gathers to a greatness, like the ooze of oil
> Crushed.[1]

---

1. Gerard Manley Hopkins, *Poems and Prose* (New York: Penguin Classics, 1985), 14.

*The world is charged with the grandeur of God.* What a pithy summary of Psalm 19:1: "The heavens declare the glory of God; the skies proclaim the work of his hands."

All these years later, whether I'm washing dishes with ample water at my kitchen sink or sitting on the back deck enjoying a late summer dinner with my family, I'll pause to watch a gorgeous sunset in silence, sharing a moment of artistic appreciation with God.

*Wow, God, you're doing it again. And I get to watch.*

What a gift.

## An Awe-Deprived Generation

While I'm grateful for my childhood, I'm not raising my children in a cabin near the woods. You really don't have to move halfway around the world to experience daily awe and wonder. You just need eyes opened to God's bountiful gifts all around you.

But we miss so much, glued as we are to our devices. We live in the most technologically advanced generation that's ever walked this earth, we've become enslaved to digital devices, and we're more sad, depressed, and sick than ever before.

Americans today spend between seven to ten hours staring at a screen each day.[2] And teenagers spend the equivalent of a forty-hour work week gaming, texting, and posting on social media—that's not even counting the time they spend on screens for education.[3]

---

2. According to a 2016 Nielsen Total Audience Report, that number is more than ten, while others report as low as seven hours a day: "Americans Devote More Than 10 Hours a Day to Screen Time, and Growing," Penn State University, February 21, 2018, https://sites.psu.edu/ist110pursel/2018/02/21/americans-devote-more-than-10-hours-a-day-to-screen-time-and-growing/.

3. "The Common Sense Census: Media Use by Tweens and Teens 2021," Common Sense Media, March 9, 2022, https://www.commonsensemedia.org/research/the-common-sense-census-media-use-by-tweens-and-teens-2021.

I'd be a hypocrite to criticize technology without acknowledging that it's these networks that enable me to serve thousands of people around the world from my little desk in northeast Ohio. Honestly, receiving emails from readers as far as the Polynesian Islands actually stirs up wonder at what God can do through technology that's surrendered to Him. Sixteen-year-old Asheritah could have never imagined the opportunities for ministry that God would open up through the advent of the internet.

But we can't ignore the cost of this connection.

Rates of depression, anxiety, and sleep disruption are skyrocketing among college students.[4] Those born in and after 1996 "are suffering from anxiety, depression, self-harm, and related disorders at levels higher than any other generation for which we have data."[5] And a recent study revealed that the youngest workers entering the workforce (Gen Z and Millennials) are "missing the equivalent of one day's work every week due to mental health concerns."[6]

While many factors contribute to these startling statistics, there's a direct correlation between the rise of technology and the decline of mental health, relational connectedness, and hope for the future.[7]

In response to these depressing statistics, parenting experts are advising young people to get outdoors for two to three hours a

4. Ahmed K. Ibrahim et al., "A Systematic Review of Studies of Depression Prevalence in University Students," *Journal of Psychiatric Research* 47, no. 3 (2013): 391–400, https://www.sciencedirect.com/science/article/pii/S0022395612003573.

5. Jonathan Haidt, "End the Phone-Based Childhood Now," *Atlantic*, March 13, 2024, https://www.theatlantic.com/technology/archive/2024/03/teen-childhood-smartphone-use-mental-health-effects/677722/.

6. Orianna Rosa Royle, "Gen Z Employees Are Missing Work for Mental Health Reasons," *Fortune*, January 24, 2024, https://fortune.com/europe/2024/01/24/gen-z-employees-missing-work-mental-health-vitality-research.

7. US Department of Health & Human Services, "The Surgeon General's Advisory on the Importance of Social Connection," https://www.hhs.gov/sites/default/files/surgeon-general-social-connection-advisory.pdf.

day—a surprisingly difficult task for today's children *and* their parents. I've recently stumbled upon the #1000hours movement: a challenge for children and grown-ups to spend 1,000 hours together outdoors each year for our mental, emotional, physical, and spiritual well-being. I've recently started tracking our outdoor hours too, because I'm always up for a challenge, and unless I'm intentionally creating time and space for us to be outside, I can go days without sniffing the fresh air outside my garage.

Because, as James Clear says, we don't rise to our goals, we fall to the level of our systems.[8] Unless we create regular rhythms—a "system," to use Clear's phrasing—to counteract the pull of our screens and step out into the grandeur of God's creation, we'll default to our habitual behavior. And as our worlds shrink to the size of our phones, our capacity to see and receive God's gifts seems to shrink as well.

We miss out on awe because we're too busy to pause and wonder at the world around us, and we're too afraid of boredom, so we swipe on our phones in search of the next dopamine hit, our gazes glued to a glowing screen.

## How Awe Heals Our Bodies and Souls

But what if boredom is actually the gateway into curiosity and wonder?

What if we stopped looking down at worthless things and started looking up to see—really *see*—the world around us?

Science seems to suggest *wonder would change our lives*. In recent years, researchers have become increasingly interested in the

---

8. James Clear, "You Do Not Rise to the Level of Your Goals. You Fall to the Level of Your Systems," https://jamesclear.com/quotes/you-do-not-rise-to-the-level-of-your-goals-you-fall-to-the-level-of-your-systems.

emotion of awe, specifically as it relates to how it affects our brains and bodies.

In a 2021 study, participants took weekly fifteen-minute walks for eight weeks. The walkers were split into two groups: the first group simply went for a walk, while researchers described the emotion of awe to the second group of walkers and suggested they try to experience that emotion by taking photographs or focusing on their surroundings rather than themselves.

Both groups of walkers experienced positive effects from their excursions, but the "awe walkers" experienced a *significantly* higher increase in positive emotions and decrease in anxiety and depression. They also described a growing sense of wonder for the world around them, not just when they were walking, but during other times of the week as well, as they'd suddenly notice "the beautiful fall colors and the absence of them amidst the evergreen forest . . . how the leaves were no longer crunchy underfoot because of the rain and how the walk was more spongy . . . the wonder that a small child feels as they explore their expanding world."[9]

A 2022 study created a model showing how "awe experiences" like spending intentional time in nature lead to increased oxytocin, increased social integration, as well as a quieting realization of how small we are in the grander scheme of things, which increases the sense of meaning and living for a greater purpose.

This finding agreed with a 2019 study that revealed that spending time in nature "can be a way to induce awe," and makes people both happier and kinder. In other words, getting outside to

9. V. E. Sturm et al, "Big Smile, Small Self: Awe Walks Promote Prosocial Positive Emotions in Older Adults," *Emotion* 22, no. 5 (2022): 1044–1058, https://psycnet .apa.org/doiLanding?doi=10.1037%2Femo0000876.

experience the grandeur of God can counterbalance the soul-numbing effects of too much time spent on screens. Perhaps this is because, according to researchers, "one of the things that may come from awe is the feeling that the individual is part of a much bigger whole."[10]

Ponder that observation for a moment: learning to slow down and notice the beauty in God's created world makes us feel both our smallness and God's greatness. Ironically, coming to grips with our finitude brings relief and peace to both our bodies and minds. We don't need to be omnipresent to the world through our phones; we don't need to comment on every news story or celebrity development; we don't need to post pictures of every meal, every leaf, or every sacred moment.[11] As we gaze out on a lake, or walk past sentinel pines, we're reminded that God has the whole world in His hands, and He's got us too. We can just be still and receive the gift of His greatness and competence at running the world—so we don't have to.

But "awe experiences"[12] don't just increase our relational intelligence and mental health, they also improve our cardiovascular health and even our lifespans. Medical researchers have studied and confirmed how these awe experiences can decrease stress, anxiety, depression, PTSD, headaches, sleep issues, body aches, digestive issues, and autoimmune disease.[13]

10. Kirsten Weir, "Nurtured by Nature," American Psychological Association (Vol. 51, No. 3), April 1, 2020, https://www.apa.org/monitor/2020/04/nurtured-nature.

11. There's a difference between taking photos to better "see" the world for the sake of appreciating the details, and actually posting those photos to garner likes and validation. We don't have to post pictures for the experience to "count."

12. Maria Monroy and Dacher Keltner, "Awe as a Pathway to Mental and Physical Health," *Perspectives on Psychological Science: A Journal of the Association for Psychological Science* 18, no. 2 (2023): 309–20, doi:10.1177/17456916221094856.

13. Ibid.

Whoa. If there were a pill that could deliver these benefits on a consistent basis, it would be flying off the shelves.[14] Yet, God created us both with the capacity to experience awe and wonder and the ability to receive His healing and joy in simple daily activities like going for a stroll in the woods or snuggling a baby in your church's nursery—so long as we remain present and engaged.[15]

**We need eyes open to see and hearts open to receive God's gifts in the world around us if we're to experience the healing power of awe and wonder.**

Obviously, the current mental health crisis facing our current generation is more complex than any one factor, and will require a multi-pronged approach to move toward healing and restoration, but one step that all experts agree on, according to the American Psychological Association: "Exposure to nature has been linked to a host of benefits, including improved attention, lower stress, better mood, reduced risk of psychiatric disorders and even upticks in empathy and cooperation."[16] And "evidence that contact with nature is associated with increases in happiness, subjective well-being, positive affect, positive social interactions and a sense of meaning and purpose in life, as well as decreases in mental distress."[17]

14. Studies have shown that something akin to awe can be experienced through psychedelics, which may explain part of its appeal (and addiction) to a generation bereft of awe-some and wonder-full experiences in their ordinary day-to-day life. See Monroy and Keltner's "Awe as a Pathway to Mental and Physical Health."

15. "Oxytocin: the Love Hormone," Harvard Health Publishing, https://www.health.harvard.edu/mind-and-mood/oxytocin-the-love-hormone.

16. Kirsten Weir, "Nurtured by Nature," *American Psychological Association* 51, no. 3 (2020): 50, https://www.apa.org/monitor/2020/04/nurtured-nature.

17. Ibid.

The reason I've specifically highlighted wonder in nature here is because there really are no scientific studies exploring the effect of wonder when we recognize God's power at work in our ordinary lives. It's just not a topic that seems to interest academia. But those of us who belong to Jesus can apply what we learn about wonder and awe in nature and look for patterns in our lives where God works in similar ways.

We need eyes open to see and hearts open to receive God's gifts in the world around us if we're to experience the healing power of awe and wonder. I don't know about you, but I've gone for walks around the neighborhood that have left my heart pumping and my breath hitching, without experiencing the benefits these researchers have talked about because going for a walk was yet another item on my to-do list. In an anxious, productivity-first mode, we're like the group of walkers who went on their stroll without purposefully searching for or experiencing awe. There's some benefit to moving your body, yes, but we're missing the hidden potential that God wants to offer us if we would just slow down to see and receive.

## Delighting in the Gifts of God

What if we stopped rushing and slowed down long enough to notice God's wonderful gifts in the ordinary moments, to marvel at the greatness of His love toward us?

Standing on the edge of the Grand Canyon inspires awe and wonder, as does standing in a grove of giant sequoia trees. But again, you don't have to travel the world to experience wonder: every spring, I'm overcome by admiration when our neighborhood magnolia trees burst into blooms of pinks and purples and creams, their beauty accented by their brevity.

Wonder is delighting in the gifts of God, knowing that these gifts reveal the love of a God who delights in us. Oftentimes, it's gifts found in His magnificent creation—free to see and enjoy all around us. Sometimes, it's gifts that are *wonderful* not because of how exquisite they are, but how very personal they are—a heartfelt desire that only your heavenly Father would know about.

Think back and consider: When have you last felt awe and wonder in your life? Where were you? What caused this emotional response? What did it feel like in your body? What thoughts came to mind?

Our souls experience wonder in something as common as holding a baby and something as rare as a solar eclipse. We respond with wonder to a symphonic orchestra and also to a toddler reciting her ABCs.

The first time I held each of my children in my arms, I cried tears of joy, amazement, and wonder—it felt like sacred space, when heaven and earth overlapped in a moment of sublime.

Wonder is the reminder that there is sacred beauty all around us, nurtured by a heavenly Father who loves us. If only we have eyes to see.

What if we learned to reflect on our day and ponder: "Where have I seen God's fingerprints today?"

## Responding to God with Wonder and Worship

What I'm suggesting here is not simply unplugging from our phones for a few minutes each day or adding "go on a weekly nature walk" to our to-do list, because it's not just *what* we do, but *how* we do it: we want to learn these rhythms of delighting *in Jesus* by becoming aware of His presence with us, within us, and all around us. And not just His presence, but specifically the markings of His presence, the telltale signs that He's been here,

He's at work here, He's left His fingerprints as a reminder of His grace here.

As we've seen throughout these Rhythms of Delight, God wants to restore our joy through the regular practice of rhythms that awaken our senses to His presence and power in the world, and in our lives too. We want to learn to recognize, appreciate, and enjoy the gifts He gives us every day, as little tokens of His affection and attention toward us.

We hear Him *Whisper*, "This is a gift for you," as we watch the sun dip toward the horizon.

We respond to Him with *Worship* and adoration, recalling to mind the *Words* of Scripture that help us interpret our experiences in light of the beautiful revelations of who God is and how He displays His glory for us all to see:

> From the rising of the sun to the place where it sets,
>    the name of the LORD is to be praised.
> The LORD is exalted over all the nations,
>    his glory above the heavens.
> *Who is like the LORD our God,*
>    the One who sits enthroned on high,
> who stoops down to look
>    on the heavens and the earth? (Psalm 113:3–6)

We marvel and *Wonder* at a God who would personally reach out to us through a thousand little gifts like this. These rhythms weave in and out of each other, enlightening us to see God's goodness as we *Walk* in step with His Spirit.

In my Bible, next to Psalm 113, I had penned these words attributed to C. S. Lewis; though I can't track them down to him in my research, it sounds like something he would say: "All joy is a gift from God, and tells a sliver of the story of who He is and what

He is like." Notice that sandwiched in the middle of the verses in the psalm above is this resounding question: "Who is like the LORD our God?" All joy is a gift from God, and every gift whispers something of His grace.

Look for ways that God may be expressing His love toward you through the acts of others. Did the car in front of you pay for your coffee order on the very day you were celebrating something with Jesus? Consider it His act of service expressing love toward you through another. Or perhaps a double rainbow graced the skies on a day you needed to be reminded of His faithfulness to keep His promises? Why wouldn't it be just for you, that you might know who He is? He loves you just that much, and He delights in you, His cherished child.

As James, the brother of Jesus, attests: "Every good and perfect gift is from above, coming down from the Father of the heavenly lights, who does not change like shifting shadows" (James 1:17). If my baby's giggle brings me so much joy, what does that tell me about God, the Giver of this gift?

Ponder that question for a moment: When you consider the many gifts which God has lavished upon you, both the eternal riches in Christ Jesus and the fleeting moments of joy in this physical world, what do these gifts reveal about the One who delights in showering you with these gifts?

Who is this God, who lavishes His children with daily joys?

## Seeing Wonder in the Ordinary

I've been slow to believe that God would take such a personal interest in me that He would orchestrate details in my life simply to communicate His love toward me.

I'd been so afraid to treat God as a genie in a bottle that I used to shrug off little things as "coincidence," as if sparing God's greatness with a logical explanation.[18] But as my children grew, I found my-self looking for opportunities to surprise them with little things I knew would delight them, whether a box of donuts on a regular Thursday or an extra round of hugs and snuggles after they'd al-ready gone to bed. I grew into the truth that "it's more blessed to give than to receive" because my heart expanded with joy every time I saw their smiles.[19]

And if we, as fallible humans, delight in lavishing gifts on our children, how much more does our heavenly Father relish the joy of surprising us with gifts too? Jesus says as much when He explains the dynamic of prayer to His disciples: "If you, then, though you are evil, know how to give good gifts to your children, *how much more will your Father in heaven give good gifts to those who ask him!*" (Matthew 7:11).

*How much more,* Jesus asks.

The answer is "immeasurably more than all we ask or imagine," once we learn to see (see Ephesians 3:20–21). Our minds cannot comprehend the magnitude of God's delight in showering us with joys great and small. He's not like a begrudging father who picks out the cheapest toy in the dollar store to do his duty; He's like a father who painstakingly crafts a custom-designed toy, sparing no expense, to communicate His great love to His child.

Our impulse to bless our loved ones echoes the heart of God to-ward us, *His* loved ones. When we look for signs of God's goodness

---

18. Up until a few years ago, I used to scoff at people who would claim that delightful surprises were God's personal gifts to them. It seemed somehow too close to the pros-perity gospel, too much like a genie-in-a-bottle approach to expressing wishes in prayer. And then I read what Jesus said in Matthew 7, and I began seeing it in my own life as a parent, and I finally conceded: God really does delight in giving His children gifts. And it causes such wonder in my heart that He would concern Himself with our little heartfelt desires.

19. See Acts 20:35.

in our world, we learn to see His signature in creation and His fingerprints in little coincidences, a flourish of clues pointing back to Him.

I finally embraced this truth a few months into my journey of asking God to restore my joy when a bouquet of flowers arrived on my doorstep. I'd succumbed to Instagram envy when I'd seen a few of my friends post photos of gorgeous arrangements from this one flower delivery company in particular. This company sourced their flowers from exotic locations and arranged them with artistic touch. *I wish I'd get a bouquet from there*, I'd sigh wistfully, as I'd swipe to the next square on the app. But the price tag on these deliveries was exorbitant, and I finally made peace with the fact that it would never happen.

Until it did.

One warm spring day, I opened my front door to find a long rectangular box with this company's logo on the side. *No way*, I breathed, as I bent low to pick it up. It felt like a dream, honestly, as I cut the box open and pulled the tissue back to reveal the colorful stems. *How could this be happening?* It wasn't just the fact that someone sent me flowers, which on its own was extremely special; it was the fact that the flowers came from the very company I'd secretly been wishing for.

"Only You, Jesus," I whispered into my empty kitchen as I carefully pulled the bouquet out of the box. "Only You could have done this." The tag on the flowers had a note and a name on it, so I texted my thoughtful friend a photo and a heartfelt thank you. On a whim, I also added, "This might seem silly, but I'd secretly wished for flowers from this company for years. You have no idea how special this is for me."

Within minutes she texted back, "Oh, how funny. The company I usually order from was experiencing an outage, so I tried this one instead. I'm glad you like them."

Like them? I loved them. And the fact that God orchestrated this friend's thoughtfulness by rerouting her order to this particular flower company? It only made this display of lavish love that much more touching. "How much more will your Father in heaven give good gifts to those who ask him?" Jesus' words echoed in my heart.

So much more. *This* much more.

*Wow, God, You did this. For me.*

*What a gift.*

## Open the Eyes of My Heart, Lord

But truth be told, I don't always see evidence of God's goodness in my life. Sometimes, the hard, the heavy, and the broken are just too much. The shattered pieces speak more to a world that's groaning for restoration than a world declaring God's eternal power and divine nature.[20] And all the walks in the woods can't seem to break through the weight of it all.

It's in those moments that I need God to open my eyes to see what's invisible to me.

"Show me your glory," I plead, like Moses in Exodus 33. And every time, God responds, "I will cause my goodness to pass before you" because God's glory is revealed in His goodness (see Exodus 33:18–23). He shows me how He pours out mercy and grace over my family in big and small ways, and it's in those times when His presence seems absent that I need Him to do the impossible and *make me see*:

> I pray that *the eyes of your heart may be enlightened* in order that you may know the hope to which he has called you, the

---

20. See Romans 8:22 and 1:20, respectively.

*riches of his glorious inheritance* in his holy people, and *his incomparably great power* for us who believe. That power is the same as the mighty strength he exerted when he raised Christ from the dead and seated him at his right hand in the heavenly realms. (Ephesians 1:18–20)

Show me Your glory, I cry. And He shows me His goodness.

Show me Your greatness, I pray. And He shows me His power in creation.

Show me Your love, I ask. And He shows me Jesus.

He opens my eyes, and I see His personal kindness in a bouquet of flowers. He opens my eyes, and I see His power in the explosive beauty of a lightning-charged sky. He opens my eyes, and I see His provision in the meal dropped off on our doorstep, the hands and feet of Jesus serving me, my Good Shepherd holding me, even as I held my baby in the NICU.

He opens my eyes, and I can finally see His presence all around me.

And when He enlightens the eyes of my heart to see and savor His glory, His greatness, and His love in my life, how else can I respond but with wonder and worship?

> The Lord has done great things for us,
>     and *we are filled with joy....*
> Those who sow with tears
>     will *reap with songs of joy.*
> Those who go out weeping,
>     carrying seed to sow,
> will *return with songs of joy,*
>     carrying sheaves with them. (Psalm 126:3–6)

When we learn to see God's great gifts of grace in our lives, we marvel at such a personal and loving God who sees us, who knows us, and who cares for us. We look at the world around us, the details of our lives, and we think, *God is doing this, and we get to watch Him do it.*

We wonder at His love, and He restores our joy.

# CHAPTER 12

# Practicing Jesus' Rhythm of Wonder

M ommy, Mommy!" My four-year-old son ran into the kitchen at perilous speed, his socked feet gliding across the wooden floor as he came to a stop beside me.

Alarmed, I dropped the dish sponge and turned toward him, but he was already tugging on my arm. "Come on," he insisted.

Heart racing, I gripped his hand and followed his lead. "What's wrong?" I gasped. "What happened?" Visions of broken bones and bloodied shins flashed across my mind, but I shoved them aside as I took a deep breath to calm my anxious heart.

"Come on!" he cried, pulling me toward the sliding deck door. I let go of his hand and sprinted across the deck and into our backyard, only to turn in a circle, puzzled. There was no one there.

"What?" I asked. "Who's hurt?" I surveyed the yard again. Nothing.

"Look!" he cried, pointing to the sky in the distance. "The sunset."

I lifted my gaze from the grassy yard to the western sky beyond. The sun outlined puffy clouds in gold as it started its slow descent on the horizon. I sighed, mesmerized by God's artistry once again on display, my heart rate coming down as the adrenaline ebbed.

A tiny hand found mine, and I kneeled by my son's side, gaze transfixed on the glorious light show.

"You love sunsets," he whispered. "And I didn't want you to miss it."

## Becoming like Little Children

We can learn so much from children.

Kids naturally go through their days with wide-eyed wonder and curiosity at this magnificent world we live in. Every day is an adventure; every tree is a portal into make-believe; every bug is an opportunity to look at the world from a different perspective, that of the miraculous ordinary.

Little ones offer fistfuls of dandelions as beautiful bouquets, and we receive the wilting weeds with earnest appreciation, never once questioning their intrinsic value: it's a precious gift precisely because of who gifted it.

There's an innocence to childhood that we know to protect as long as possible. There's an exuberance to childhood that we think back on with fondness. And there's a posture of wonder to childhood that we can recapture if we desire.

I see all this in my own kids, and I'm reminded of Jesus' admonishment to "change and become like little children," perhaps in this way, among others (see Matthew 18:1–5).

What would it look like to become like children in the way we engage with the natural world around us? What would it look like to have the faith to see and receive God's gifts of grace for us?

How can you bring back this childlike delight into your structured time with Jesus this week? If you're not sure what that looks like, ponder this: What did the five-year-old version of yourself enjoy doing most? Was it painting? Dancing? Singing at the top of your lungs? Playing outside? Looking at the clouds? Incorporate that element of joy and delight back into your devotional life, at least once this week, if not more.

I think of Jesus gathering the little ones in His lap, praying a blessing over them, and turning to His disciples with the warning, "Truly I tell you, anyone who will not receive the kingdom of God like a little child will never enter it" (Luke 18:17).

How can we help but respond: *In that case, Lord, teach me how to receive Your kingdom like a little child. Reawaken my sense of wonder. Stir up my curiosity and faith. Help me believe and receive what You want to offer me.*

*Show me how to live a life of wonder, like Jesus did.*

## Jesus Recognized God's Hand at Work in Wonder

There are some people who claim that if they saw a modern-day miracle, they would believe that God truly is who He says He is and can do what He says He can do. But if part of wonder is learning to see God's greatness and love through His gifts to us, then we first need eyes that are open to recognize His hand at work around us.

### Recognize the miracles

Jesus faced a crowd demanding a display of His miraculous power in order to believe, and He lamented their unbelief: "For if the miracles that were performed in you had been performed in Tyre and Sidon, they would have repented long ago in sackcloth and ashes" (Matthew 11:21). They had seen Jesus perform miracles, they had witnessed the wonders of His power, and they still did not believe (see also John 15:24–25). But the humble heart always seeks to see the glory of God in all things great and small.

Jesus recognized His Father's hand at work through His miracles, and we can follow His example by recognizing the wonders of God that flowed through Jesus in the Gospels and continue to flow through Him in the world today too. Let us be the first to ascribe to God the wonder of a miraculous healing in the hospital, a miraculous reconciliation among family members, a miraculous provision for exactly what we need. God still works miracles today.

### Praise God for revealing Himself

On the heels of this lament, Jesus turns His heart toward praise:

> At that time Jesus said, "I praise you, Father, Lord of heaven and earth, because you have hidden these things from the wise and learned, and revealed them to little children. Yes, Father, for this is what you were pleased to do.
> All things have been committed to me by my Father. No one knows the Son except the Father, and no one knows the Father except the Son and those to whom the Son chooses to reveal him." (Matthew 11:25–27)

Did you catch that? Jesus rejoiced that His Father *was pleased* to reveal hidden things to those followers who were like "little children." And what things did the Father reveal? The hidden things of Jesus. Don't miss this: God delights to reveal the riches of Christ Jesus to His children who believe (see Ephesians 3:8).

### Learn more about the wonder of Jesus

This is our entryway into wonder: it's choosing to believe, to recognize, and to receive what God desires to offer us in Christ Jesus.

First and foremost, more of Himself. The greatest riches of heaven are not health, wealth, and prosperity; the greatest riches of heaven are deeper revelations into the mystery of the Father in Jesus Christ. In a very similar passage, after Jesus' disciples return to Him celebrating the miraculous wonders they had performed in His name, Jesus responds:

> At that time Jesus, *full of joy through the Holy Spirit*, said, "I praise you, Father, Lord of heaven and earth, because you have hidden these things from the wise and learned, and revealed them to little children. Yes, Father, for *this is what you were pleased to do.*
>
> "All things have been committed to me by my Father. No one knows who the Son is except the Father, and no one knows who the Father is except the Son *and those to whom the Son chooses to reveal him.*"
>
> Then he turned to his disciples and said privately, "*Blessed are the eyes that see what you see.* For I tell you that many prophets and kings wanted to see what you see but did not see it, and to hear what you hear but did not hear it."
> (Luke 10:21–24)

Notice how Jesus celebrated, full of joy, the things that brought His heavenly Father pleasure: that is, the revelation of the Son through the Spirit to those whose eyes were open to see and receive Him.

On this increasing revelation, Jesus said:

> "I have much more to say to you, *more than you can now bear.* But when he, the Spirit of truth, comes, *he will guide you into all the truth.* He will not speak on his own; he will speak only what he hears, and he will tell you what is yet to come. He will glorify me because *it is from me that he will receive what he will make known to you.*" (John 16:12–14)

One of the greatest gifts God desires to give us, aside from eternal salvation and adoption into His family, is an ever-deepening revelation of who Jesus is. Think about that: God is pleased to reveal Himself to His children through His Spirit's revelation of His Son.

As you consider your personal knowledge of Jesus, are you growing to know Him more every month? Every year? Have you discovered new things about Him in His Word that could only be revealed to you through the work of His Spirit making it known to you?

### Practice the Rhythm of Wonder through the Daily Examen

One way we can grow in wonder over who Jesus is and how He's at work in the world is through a practice called the Daily Examen.

A short reflection at the end of the day, we recall in our mind's eye the events of the past twenty-four hours. We become aware of God's presence with us through His Spirit, and we ask Him to open our eyes to recognize His hand at work. Then we prayerfully consider where we felt most close to Him during that day. When was His comforting presence most evident during our daily activities? We ask Him to show us when we missed what He was wanting to do with us, or when we were running away from His presence, or ignoring His prompts in our lives. We look for evidence of God's blessings, for the pattern of His fingerprints, for the whisper of His love.

> When we develop a rhythm of reviewing our days with Jesus, we learn to recognize His hand at work in our every day.

Where He convicts us of sin, we repent and ask forgiveness.

Where He comforts us with His nearness, we rejoice.

Where He reveals to us an aspect of His character, we test it against Scripture and receive it.

I practice this rhythm in a simpler way with my children, in what we call "Two Roses and a Thorn." Around the dinner table most nights, I'll prompt them to share two wonderful experiences and one hard one, and sometimes we look at how God's hand was at work in all those situations. It's a simple but effective way to help children visualize God's invisible presence in their lives.

When we develop a rhythm of reviewing our days with Jesus, we learn to recognize His hand at work in our every day, so we can more quickly discern His presence in the present moment.

## Jesus Thanked God for His Gifts

Another aspect of wonder is not only recognizing but receiving God's gifts with thanksgiving. As we look at the life of Jesus, we see a pattern of gratitude and thankfulness in big and little things.

Not only did Jesus thank His Father for revealing hidden things to His children, He also gave thanks before miraculously multiplying the bread and the fish, before raising Lazarus from the dead, and before breaking bread and sharing the wine at His final Passover (John 6:10; 11:41–42; Luke 22:17–19). Thanksgiving always precedes the miracle, because responding to God in/with gratitude is part of the Rhythm of Wonder.

In our own lives, we can keep a record of God's gifts in our lives to help us recognize and respond with thanksgiving. Whether you keep a numbered journal counting up to 1,000 like author Ann Voskamp and others have done over the years, or you simply start each day by counting your blessings, incorporating thanksgiving into your day will not only make you more grateful, it will increase both your wonder and your joy.[1]

---

1. "Giving Thanks Can Make You Happier," Harvard Health Publishing, August 14, 2021, https://www.health.harvard.edu/healthbeat/giving-thanks-can-make-you-happier.

## Jesus Created and Sustains the Wonder of Creation

As fully God and fully human, Jesus interacted with the world in ways that are both similar to and different from us. We'll look at a range of Jesus' wonder in the Gospels, especially how He related to the natural world, and see how we may learn to follow His example.

While we venture into God's wonderful world with curiosity and awe, Jesus walked the earth as the One who created it all: "Through him all things were made; without him nothing was made that has been made" (John 1:3).

Consider also Colossians 1:16: "For everything was created by him, in heaven and on earth, the visible and the invisible . . . all things have been created through him and for him" (CSB). If we look up at the stars and marvel at the expanse of the universe, imagine Jesus' delight in the stars He shaped with the sound of His voice!

We know that Jesus delighted in the work of His hands because it's right there in the beginning: "God saw all that he had made, and *it was very good*" (Genesis 1:31). The preincarnate Christ was pleased with His handiwork at the beginning of creation; what must His experience have been like to enter this world and walk among His created? "For in him we live and move and have our being" (Acts 17:28). The miracle of Christmas is the infinite God taking on finite human flesh to become one of us.

## Jesus Walked Among His Created

The focus of the gospel narratives is not on providing a complete biographical account of every single one of Jesus' thoughts, feelings, and experiences, but on showing us the good news of the gospel. Therefore, we're not told what it was like for Jesus to walk along the banks of the Jordan River and watch the rippling current carrying leaves downstream. We aren't told what He thought or felt when

He rested under a leafy tree on a sweltering day. I've endeavored to stay within the guardrails of orthodoxy and healthy hermeneutics, while also extending just a bit of sanctified imagination when pondering Jesus' experience of being fully human. Marvel with me, then, at the undeniable reality: God Himself walking among His image bearers, the Creator among His created.

Without the convenience of vehicles, Jesus spent hours of His life walking hundreds of miles in His three years of ministry. This would have given Him ample time to admire His handiwork in creation, whether out in the Judean mountains or out in the middle of a lake.[2] Jesus also often withdrew to the wilderness to pray, to be alone with His heavenly Father, and to be refreshed (see Luke 5:16).[3]

Though Jesus traveled a lot during His earthly ministry, He didn't road trip to explore the natural wonders of the world; instead, He lived and traveled in a roughly ninety-mile radius of His hometown, appreciating the beauty of the created world wherever His ministry took Him.

### The delight of a daily walk

As a missionary kid who's crossed the Atlantic a dozen times, I'm naturally inclined toward wanderlust. I spend my free time dreaming and planning road trips for my family as we hope to visit the US national parks before our children launch on their own. But I need this reminder to tap into the Rhythm of Wonder available

---

2. Jesus clearly delighted in the work of His hands (see Luke 6:12, Mark 1:35, and Matthew 6:28–29).

3. Also, when He was out in the wilderness with the wild beasts for forty days, how could that not have been a wonder-filled time? Consider Isaiah 43:20: "The wild animals honor me, the jackals and the owls, because I provide water in the wilderness and streams in the wasteland, to give drink to my people, my chosen," streams from which Jesus Himself would have drunk to parch His thirst.

daily in my own proverbial backyard. I don't have to cross state lines to see a breathtaking display of God's power in creation; an after-dinner stroll with my family in the neighborhood reminds me to keep my eyes and heart wide open to recognize God's gifts all around me.

### Organize nature walks

If walking outdoors is new to you, try planning a nature walk once a week with friends, or see if your county parks system hosts any challenges that you could join.[4] One of our family's favorite traditions is a fall hiking spree that takes us to new parks that we've never hiked before. It still amazes me how hiking as a family calms anxious temperaments, quiets down scuffles, and brings a spring of joy in our steps.

### Read nature-inspired poetry

Last, consider reading poetry about how God reveals Himself in nature (i.e., "God's Grandeur" by Gerard Manley Hopkins) while you're actually outside in nature; reflect on what you learn about God from these poems and how you can respond to Him with wonder and worship.

## Jesus Enjoyed the Beauty of Creation

Where the cadence of crashing waves reminds us of our finitude in the face of endless water, Jesus was the One who separated the land from the sky and placed a boundary for the ocean. Whereas the majesty of a mountain range may make us feel small

---

4. For more inspiration on organizing nature walks with friends, check out Ginny Yurich's podcast called *1,000 Hours Outside*, available wherever you listen to podcasts, and also linked in this book's resource library at delightinginjesus.com.

and fleeting, Jesus was the One who formed those mountains with a spoken "let there be."

Psalm 19:1 tells us that "the heavens declare the glory of God; the skies proclaim the work of his hands." If we can recognize the glory of God in creation, how much more would Jesus have recognized and appreciated the beauty of the world He had made?

Or consider: "For since the creation of the world God's invisible qualities—his eternal power and divine nature—have been clearly seen, being understood from what has been made" (Romans 1:20). If we can tease out aspects of God's goodness, His power, His love as we marvel at creation, how much more would Jesus have seen and recognized these things, being fully God and fully human, without the taint of sin?

As humans, we don't create like Jesus did, but do get to participate in the First Commission He gave us:

> So God created mankind in his own image,
> in the image of God he created them;
> male and female he created them.
>
> God blessed them and said to them, "Be fruitful and increase in number; fill the earth and subdue it. Rule over the fish in the sea and the birds in the sky and over every living creature that moves on the ground." (Genesis 1:27–28)

### Plant seeds to join creation's rhythm

We can join Jesus in this Rhythm of Wonder in creation not only by walking in the natural world and noting what's already there—sky, sun, clouds, trees—but also by harnessing creation's potential to create beauty and order in the pattern set by God.

We can do this in our own little corner of the world, whether it's a little yard in suburbia, spacious acreage in the country, or a little flowerpot in an apartment window. Even though I have a black thumb, snowdrops, daffodils, and tulips keep popping up in my flowerbeds each spring. This undeserved gift that returns year after year causes me to join the psalmist in declaring, "How many are your works, LORD! In wisdom you made them all; the earth is full of your creatures" (Psalm 104:24).

Receiving God's gifts in creation might look like getting out-doors every day, maybe laying down in the grass once in a while, and looking at the clouds, "the dust of God's feet" (Nahum 1:3). As we see poetic evidence of God's movement in the world, we can reflect on where God is moving in our own lives and wonder at what He might be doing.

## Jesus Paid Attention to the Wonder of Creation

Far different from the concrete jungle many of us live in today, Jesus lived in an agrarian society, spending a lot of time outdoors. Many of His parables and illustrations display attentiveness and ap-preciation for nature (consider the birds of the air and the flowers in the field in Matthew 6:25–26 and Luke 12:24; or the parable of the sower and the seed in Matthew 13:4–9).

Though He could have based His teaching ministry in syna-gogues or the temple, most often Jesus taught outside in nature, teaching and healing where anyone could have free access to Him. The Gospels often describe Him teaching from a boat on the shore of the Sea of Galilee, or out on the hillside, like when He delivered what we now call the Sermon on the Mount.

### Read the Word outside

We often read the gospel accounts indoors, in an environment far removed from the natural environment in which Jesus would have ministered. Consider reading or listening to the Sermon on the Mount outside, looking for examples around you for all the nature imagery in Jesus' teachings.

### Keep a nature journal

If you, like me, struggle to be observant about the wonder of creation, try keeping a nature journal in which you record what you see when you're out in nature. Try drawing or painting something from your observations, whether it's a landscape or a single fern frond. You might be surprised, like me, to discover how much complexity and beauty God has hidden in the smallest aspect of the created world, like a frond. The goal here is not to create masterpieces that will hang on our walls, but to discipline ourselves to actually see what's in front of us, to pay attention to the little details and the breathtaking big views.

### Learn the science behind creation from experts

Another way to cultivate attention is by learning about creation to better admire our Creator. Watch videos on macro- and microbiology; take a mini-class on astronomy; refresh your memory of anatomy with your children's biology textbooks; and let the marvel of this created world move you to wonder and worship our Creator God—who crafted the world so intricately and still cares for us so intimately.

## Jesus Demonstrated His Power over Creation

As the Creator of every atom in this universe, Jesus holds power to command creation to do what He wills. Jesus brought wholeness and healing to those who were blind, crippled, deaf, bleeding, and even dead (see Luke 7:22). Jesus guided a school of fish into Peter's net, at least twice (see Luke 5:4–5 and John 21:3–19), and multiplied bread and fish to feed a multitude (see Matthew 14:13–21).

In one of my favorite stories, Jesus spoke to a raging storm and commanded it to be still, a command the winds and the waves immediately obeyed, much to the disciples' astonishment (Mark 4:35–41 and Luke 8:22–25). It's this encounter, more than any other, that causes the disciples to tremble in appropriate fear and wonder of Him: "Who is this? Even the wind and the waves obey him!" (Mark 4:41).

### Exclaim our astonishment and awe at Jesus' power

In this instance, we can't follow Jesus' examples, but we can instead turn to the disciples, who model the appropriate response for our hearts too; when we see something *wonder*-full in creation, may it point our hearts to our Creator, the One whose power holds it all together, with humility and awe inspiring us to exclaim, as Paul did:

> The Son is the image of the invisible God, the firstborn over all creation. For *in him all things were created*: things in heaven and on earth, visible and invisible, whether thrones or powers or rulers or authorities; all things have been *created through him and for him*. He is before all things, and *in him all things hold together*. (Colossians 1:15–17)

### Sing out our wonder and awe

It is good and appropriate for our hearts to bow in humble adoration before the One who holds creation in place. We can teach our hearts to delight in Him by singing songs about God's creation that lift your heart in adoration and wonder. Here are a few of my favorites:

- "All Creatures of Our God and King"

- "How Great Thou Art"

- "I Come to the Garden Alone"

- "Great Is Thy Faithfulness"

### Jesus Marveled at People's Faith with Wonder

Last, there's only two places in the Gospels that describe Jesus as being amazed, and both times, they're connected to the absence or presence of faith.

In Mark 6, Jesus teaches with such authority that His childhood neighbors are amazed—but they refuse to believe. Mark observes: "He could not do any miracles there, except lay his hands on a few sick people and heal them. He was amazed at their lack of faith" (vv. 5–6). What started as His neighbor's amazement turned into Jesus' amazement at their lack of faith. They had every reason to believe, but they refused.

In Matthew 8, though, Jesus encounters a foreigner who had every reason to disbelieve Him, but demonstrates tremendous faith, causing Jesus to remark in amazement, "Truly I tell you, I have not found anyone in Israel with such great faith" (v. 10). How remarkable that the "pioneer and perfecter of our faith" would remark on this man's great faith (Hebrews 12:2).

I want to have the kind of faith that amazes Jesus. I want to have the childlike faith that moves Jesus to rejoice. I want to have the faith that pleases God and stirs Him to reward me with more and more: more sight, more revelation, more faith, more wonder (see Hebrews 11:1–6).

This can be one of our rhythms of wonder too. Let us become a people who experience God's healing and revealing power through wonder, learning to see and celebrate the goodness of God in all the gifts He lavishes on us—and practice great faith by believing He is who He says He is and can do what He says He will do.

Eyes to see, hearts to receive, faith to believe. This rhythm draws from our whole selves, every minute of every day.

## How Will You Delight in the Gifts of God?

I hope by now you've caught a vision for God's desire to reveal His greatness and His great love toward you through the gifts He surrounds you with every day. It's an open invitation to delight in Jesus by experiencing awe and wonder in our daily lives, as we learn to see His fingerprints in the big and little things.

As we create rhythms of wonder with Jesus, whether by discerning His work in our lives or by spending intentional time outdoors in nature, we'll witness Him restoring joy bit by bit. **Pick one of the Wonder ideas above, or come up with your own, and then make a growth plan to make it a natural part of your life in the weeks to come:**

- How will you make this Rhythm of Wonder small?

- What daily routines can you link to your wonder? "When I _____, I will _____."

- How can you make your Rhythm of Wonder fun and personal to you?

- How will you celebrate your growth each week? Month? Year?

Remember that it takes time for new rhythms to become habitual, but the more you practice with intentionality, the more naturally it will come. And try to invite other people to join you in these rhythms; not only will you find yourself more likely to stick with them, but remember that joy is relational, so you'll more likely enjoy it more too.

# CHAPTER 13

# Delighting in Obedience to God: *Walking*

*Could we go for a walk? I really need to talk to someone.* I took a few deep breaths to calm my anxious heart and hit "send" on my phone's screen.

I'd reached my lowest point, and in a moment of desperation, I texted my friend Juli, hoping she'd say yes (and not think me *too weird*).

Graciously, she agreed to meet at a local park the following week, and we walked the trail for miles, crunching colorful leaves under our boots. I told her of the burnout I was facing, the burdens I was carrying, the brokenness I felt inside. I told her I was afraid of missing God's will; I was worried that God was finished with me. We paused to listen to the honking geese migrating south for the winter, flying in V-formation overhead.

"I just wanna walk away," I confided in her as we resumed our hike. Not away from Jesus, *never*. And not away from my family.

But I'd grown weary of scandals in the church, disheartened by the constant doomsday political headlines, and exhausted by the hustle to keep up with all that was required of me. I dreamed of moving to a tropical island and escaping all my problems, but I knew they would just follow me there: I wasn't sleeping well, wasn't eating well, wasn't breathing well. I just needed someone to fix me.

Like a patient counselor, Juli listened to my rambling, interjecting only to ask questions. I hoped she'd tell me which projects to turn down or suggest a way to stay more organized as a working mom. Maybe she could share the secret to balancing all my responsibilities with a smile on my face.

"What would you do if you were in my place?" I prompted, huffing as we trekked up the hills.

But Juli evaded the question; she wouldn't tell me what to do. Instead, she walked with me through my uncertainty. She spoke wisdom, reminding me of what I knew to be true. And she told me about her shoebox: a practical way of asking God for discernment, which I'll share in the next chapter.

But more than anything, Juli reminded me of this truth: God would be faithful to walk with me into the next season of my life, whatever that looked like. And she was right.

Just a few days after that forest walk with Juli, I walked up to Carol at the conference that I wrote about at the beginning of this book. One walk led to the other, each an important step in God's work to restore the sparkle to my eyes.

## A God Who Longs to Walk with His People

Throughout history, God has always desired companionship and friendship with the humans He created in His own image. We see this from the very beginning in the garden of Eden, as Adam and Eve heard "the sound of the LORD God as he was walking in the garden in the cool of the day" (Genesis 3:8). The way the scene is described, it appears that this was a regular part of their interactions, as the couple knew to expect Him there.

God invites His people to collaborate with Him in the work He's doing in the world by obeying His whispers. I like to picture this dynamic of friendship and obedience as *Walking* with God. Every email, every conference call, every meal prepped, every floor swept has the capacity to hold divine purpose because we are divinely indwelled by God's own Spirit.[1]

Even when sin marred humans' relationship with God, He remained undeterred in His desire to walk with us. We see this in the life of Enoch, who *"walked faithfully* with God; then he was no more, because God took him away" (Genesis 5:24). And when God chose Abram to form a special covenant relationship with his family, He told Abram to *"walk* before me *faithfully"* (Genesis 17:1). In both of these men's examples, walking with God signifies a close relationship, a consistent obedience, and a mutual enjoyment of each other's presence.

God's presence went before the Israelites in the wilderness as a pillar of cloud by day and pillar of fire by night (Exodus 13:21). His presence literally illuminated the path for them, moving so they could follow Him on the next stage of their jour-

---

1. I'm fascinated by the idea that "all work is God's work." I can't recall where I first heard this phrase, but I've since learned that Tim Keller spoke about this at The Gospel Coalition's 2013 Faith at Work Post-Conference. This particular quote (which includes the words of Luther) stuck with me: "'The people who do the simplest kinds of work are actually the fingers of God.' . . . God is loving you and doing things to you, and he has chosen to do it through the work of other people. And therefore all work—all work— is actually God's work. It's God's way of caring for His creation." What a wonderful thought! Tim Keller, "All Work Is God's Work!" YouTube, August 18, 2023, https://www.youtube.com/watch?v=XosLwWER1PU.

ney and protecting them from their enemies, finally resting on the finished tabernacle to signify the place where His people could come to meet with Him (Exodus 40:36–38).

When Moses warns God's people to obey the Lord, he says "*Walk in obedience* to all that the LORD your God has commanded you" (Deuteronomy 5:33). And when God wanted to reassure them of His presence, He used this same metaphor of walking to emphasize His presence and protection: "The LORD himself *goes before you* and *will be with you*; he will never leave you nor forsake you. Do not be afraid; do not be discouraged" (Deuteronomy 31:8).

David describes his desire to walk with God even when he couldn't see the path clearly: "I *follow close* to you; your right hand holds on to me" (Psalm 63:8 CSB). Notice how David pictures God holding him by the hand to guide him, even in the darkness and in despair: "*Even though I walk* through the darkest valley, I will fear no evil, *for you are with me*" (Psalm 23:4). It's the closeness of God's presence, the reassurance of His touch, that brings comfort to our souls.

And when God called His people to repent of their sin, notice how He uses this same word picture: "He has shown you, O mortal, what is good. And what does the LORD require of you? To act justly and to love mercy and *to walk humbly with your God*" (Micah 6:8).

Our Creator God continuing to walk with His people even after their infidelity and disobedience is wonderful enough. But the shock comes when God Himself leaves the glory of heaven to take on human flesh and walk among His precious image bearers. No other deity in the imagination of humanity has ever deigned to humble themselves in the dust. But our Lord did so, out of His faithful love that would stop at nothing to restore fellowship with His humans, to make Himself known to us, that we would personally know the God who is mercy, the God who is love, and the God who is grace.[2]

---

2. See 1 Peter 1:12.

And when, enfleshed, He reaches out to invite people to Himself, it should come as no surprise that He picks up the metaphor of walking when He says to Peter, Andrew, James, and John: "Come, follow me" (Matthew 4:19).

## In the Dust of His Feet

As a rabbi, Jesus' call to "follow Him" would have sounded familiar to His listeners' ears. In Jewish tradition, this phrase was a teacher's official invitation for students to join him in apprenticeship, to learn what he knew, to do what he did, to become like him in every little thing. Some disciples even adopted their rabbi's mannerisms and way of speaking. A disciple was expected to walk so closely to his rabbi that others would send him off with the blessing: "May you be covered in the dust of your rabbi."[3]

Imagine Jesus and His twelve disciples walking mile after mile on the dusty roads of the Judean countryside, the disciples elbowing each other to get closest to Him, to catch every word He spoke, to have a chance to answer His questions, to be so close that the dust from His steps would settle on their own feet. That's the picture of a disciple walking close to their rabbi. And while being covered in dust is not an attractive proposition to our twenty-first-century, germ-averse sensibilities, walking in step with Jesus is exactly what He calls all of us to today.

Many rabbis taught strict adherence to Jewish laws and traditions, even adding to God's commands their own extra expectations. These rabbis burdened their followers with unattainable expectations, while not bothering to follow the same commands themselves (see Matthew 23:3–4). It's like going on a backpacking trip and

---

3. Lois Tverberg, "Covered in the Dust of Your Rabbi: An Urban Legend?," Our Rabbi Jesus, January 27, 2012, https://ourrabbijesus.com/covered-in-the-dust-of-your-rabbi-an-urban-legend/.

expecting someone else to carry all the heavy gear and provisions, and then adding rocks to their pack when they're not watching.

In stark contrast, Jesus looks out on a crowd of weary men and women, exhausted from carrying the burden of trying to keep the hundreds of detailed interpretations of God's laws and rabbinic traditions, and says to them:

> "Come to me, all you who are weary and burdened, and I will give you rest. Take my yoke upon you and learn from me, for I am gentle and humble in heart, and you will find rest for your souls. For my yoke is easy and my burden is light." (Matthew 11:28–30)

One thing we often miss in this beautiful invitation of Jesus is that His rest takes the form of activity, not passivity—He's calling them to walk in step with Him, to learn from Him, to work with Him. He's calling them, *us*, to step into yoke with Him.

**When Jesus invites us into His yoke, He's calling us to walk in step with Him, to follow His lead, to learn from His example, to let Him to shoulder our load.**

During my growing-up years in Romania, my grandfather was one of only two farmers in our village to own a tractor; everyone else worked their fields with ancient-looking plows pulled by two cattle who were yoked together. I spent many afternoons watching these massive creatures plod through the dusty ground, held side by side by a curved piece of wood. A yoke is a simple tool, but effective:

One creature can't race ahead of the other; they must stay in step.

One creature can't go its own way; they must walk in the same direction.

One creature doesn't have to bear the burden alone; they carry it together, but the bigger, stronger one shoulders the bulk of the load.

When Jesus invites us to step into His yoke, He's calling us to walk in step with Him, to follow His lead, to learn from His example, to let Him shoulder our load. We can rest, even as we walk, because Jesus' yoke—His interpretation of God's commands—is actually *easy*.

## The Easy Yoke of Jesus

We see how light Jesus' burden really is when He summarizes the Pharisees' many commands in two simple ones:

> "'Love the Lord your God with all your heart and with all your soul and with all your mind.' This is the first and greatest commandment. And the second is like it: 'Love your neighbor as yourself.' All the Law and the Prophets hang on these two commandments." (Matthew 22:37–40)

Compared to the complicated religious system of Jewish adherence to the law, Jesus' "yoke" of what it means to obey God is rather straightforward: love. According to Jesus, everything He did, He did out of love. To follow Him is to learn His rhythm of love ("learn from me"), to keep in step with His pace ("gentle and humble in heart"), and to walk in His acts of love in the world ("take my yoke upon you").[4]

---

4. The Bible tells us that at His very essence, God is love (1 John 4:8). Everything God has ever done has flowed out of His heart of love, and as God enfleshed in human form, Jesus lived out that love in ways people could easily see and understand. Everything Jesus did, He did out of love. He was—and remains—a living example of "the love chapter," 1 Corinthians 13, in action. I explored this way of reading the Gospels through the lens of 1 Corinthians 13 in my book *Uncovering the Love of Jesus* (Chicago: Moody Publishers, 2020).

Jesus makes this point clear in His last discourse to His disciples on the night He was betrayed:

> "As the Father has loved me, so have I loved you. Now remain in my love. If you keep my commands, you will remain in my love, just as I have kept my Father's commands and remain in his love. I have told you this so that my joy may be in you and that your joy may be complete. (John 15:9–11)

Love and joy are inextricably linked to Jesus. There is no other way to live a joyful life outside of walking in Jesus' love and walking out His love toward others, and this command to love is not overbearing, but the sharing of a plan among friends:

> "You are my friends if you do what I command. I no longer call you servants, because a servant does not know his master's business. Instead, *I have called you friends*. . . . I chose you and appointed you so that you might go and bear fruit—fruit that will last—and so that whatever you ask in my name the Father will give you. *This is my command: Love each other*." (John 15:14–17)

A life of friendship and obedience to the impulse of love. That's the core of what it means to walk in the yoke with Jesus.

When Jesus called people to "follow Him," it wasn't an invitation to identify as part of a party or tribe; it was a call to join Him in His work of love and so experience overflowing joy through our obedience.

But Jesus' disciples got to physically walk with Him and witness firsthand His works of love. How do we keep in step with Jesus when He's no longer physically walking the earth? How do we know what loving acts He's calling us to when we can't see Him or physically hear Him?

This tension is exactly why Jesus said it was better for Him to go up to His Father. Because something better was coming.

*Something better?*

## Walking in Step with God's Spirit

I was fresh out of college, reading the Bible in a new translation, when I read Jesus telling His disciples: "I tell you the truth. *It is better for you that I go away*" (John 16:7 LEB).

Wait . . . what? How could it be *better* for Jesus to go away? I didn't believe it, so I checked my usual translation; it read: "But very truly I tell you, *it is for your good* that I am going away."

But surely that couldn't be right. Wouldn't it be better for Jesus to have stayed on earth? I checked another translation, this one known for its accuracy to the original text: "Nevertheless, I tell you the truth: *it is to your advantage* that I go away" (ESV).

I settled back in my chair. How could this be?

As a teenager on fire for Jesus, I harbored some holy jealousy for those first-century disciples. I would love to have been one of the women following Him, serving Him, supporting Him with their riches. What would it have been like to hear His voice, to feel His touch, to see His smiling face?

How could it be possible that Jesus thought it better for Him to leave this earth? I kept reading: "It is to your advantage that I go away, for if I do not go away, the Helper will not come to you. But if I go, I will send him to you" (John 16:7 ESV).

*The Helper.* While Jesus walked this earth, He lived confined to one place and time, subject to the limitations of a human body. And while Jesus will never cease being human, His divine nature now dwells in His followers through His Spirit—His presence abiding within each person who bears His name. What an incredible gift!

Jesus' own Spirit acts as a seal, a down payment, and a promise of what is to come: eternal reunion with Him (see Ephesians 1:14). In the meantime, His Spirit comforts us, teaches us, guides us, energizes us, matures us, and grows His fruit of love in us, as we saw in the previous chapter.

It is Jesus' Spirit within us that empowers us to walk in His love, turning away from the lure of sin and stepping into the freedom of life with Him: "*Walk by the Spirit*, and you will not gratify the desires of the flesh" (Galatians 5:16). And just a few verses later, we read: "Since we live by the Spirit, let us keep in step with the Spirit" (Galatians 5:25).

## Joining God's Spirit in His Work in the World

Life with God is not about chasing mountaintop experiences we encounter at conferences or retreats, nor is it about flashy spirituality that makes the headlines; discipleship to Jesus is best seen as "a long obedience in the same direction," as Eugene Peterson described it.[5] Walking in the Spirit, day by day.

It's a lifetime of consistency and patience, of learning about Him in the Word and responding to Him in worship, of listening to God's *Whisper* and obeying Him in your *Walk*, and then *Wondering* at the work of His Spirit in you, through you, and around you. This isn't a ten-step program with a quick result or your money back; this is life with Jesus, in step with His Spirit, going where He goes and doing what He does.

Because of Jesus' Spirit living inside us, we no longer have to rely on our own limited willpower or motivation to try to please God or live inside His will. God invites us to join Him in what He

---

5. Eugene Peterson, *A Long Obedience in the Same Direction: Discipleship in an Instant Society* (Westmont, IL: InterVarsity Press, 2019).

is about in the world, by empowering us through His own Spirit to accomplish that work. The Spirit who raised Jesus from the dead is living inside each of us who follows Him (see Romans 8:10–11). Think of that: God doesn't work in disembodied ways in the world; God works through the body of Christ, which you're part of if you belong to Jesus.

And Jesus promised that His Spirit would energize us for incredible works, because He Himself promises to participate as well:

> "Very truly I tell you, whoever believes in me *will do the works I have been doing*, and *they will do even greater things than these*, because I am going to the Father. And I will do whatever you ask in my name, so that the Father may be glorified in the Son. You may ask me for anything in my name, and *I will do it.*" (John 14:12–14)

Greater things than what Jesus did? That's wild to think about, but it's Jesus' own promise, extended not just to His eleven disciples, but to all of us who believe and follow Him.

Notice the connection between us doing works at the beginning, and Jesus doing the work—"I will do it"—in response to our prayers. These Rhythms of Delight all weave together in a life lived in friendship with God.

God's own Spirit lives inside us, empowering us, and Jesus Himself intercedes for us, so that our Father would work in such incredible ways in us that people would "see [our] good deeds and glorify [our] Father in heaven" (Matthew 5:16).

We need not live mediocre, defeated, boring lives when God invites us into so much more!

# Common Obstacles to Walking with God (and How to Overcome Them)

Walking with God presupposes we're listening to His whisper and staying in step with His pace. At times, though, we walk in accordance with what we hear but get tripped up.

## We don't "feel" God, so we assume He's not with us.

Because we don't see God with our physical eyes or hear Him with our physical ears, we struggle to feel like He's with us.

But our physical bodies are just one aspect of who we are. God created us body, mind, and spirit, and we need to develop our capacity to perceive with our spiritual senses as well. This is why Paul prays for the Ephesians that "the eyes of [their] heart may be enlightened" (Ephesians 1:18); we would do well to pray the same. God is Spirit, so are you learning to listen with your spirit to His?

## We're overwhelmed by our own to-do lists, so we resist adding anything else.

We're so busy paying our bills, pursuing our dreams, and living our life that the thought of God adding to our already-full plate feels overwhelming. Who has time for more activities when we're already exhausted trying to keep up with what we're already doing?

Remember, God isn't a demanding taskmaster or Pharisee, laying heavy burdens onto our already stooped shoulders. Rather, He's the One who invites us to lay down those burdens and step into the yoke with Jesus. When we ask God to rule over our schedules, our to-do lists, and our goals and dreams, we'll learn to discern what actually needs done, and what's just keeping us busy. We'll find that He only ever gives us what we can achieve through His power at work in us through His Spirit.

We don't believe God's actually interested in us, so we forge ahead alone.

When we hear of God working in amazing ways, we assume that's just for missionaries, pastors, and spiritual giants. We're not that important to God, we think; He hasn't done those mighty works *through us*, so He must not really care about us that way.

There are no spare parts in the body of Christ. From the very beginning, God's purpose has always worked through humans to accomplish His work in the world, and because Jesus conquered sin and death, He has made us "to be a kingdom and priests to serve our God, and [we] will reign on the earth" with Him (see Revelation 5:9–10). That work begins here and now, with each one who belongs to Him.

We don't obey what He's already revealed to us, so we don't hear His voice.

At some point in our lives, we've waited to hear from God on something big, only to be disappointed. Whether we were looking for a spouse, a job, a move, or something else, we heard nothing. We assume that means God doesn't do that for us (as said above).

If we want to hear God's voice in the big things, we must be quick to obey Him in the little things. He won't reveal new things until we obey what He's already revealed.[6] It took me literal *years* to really grasp this truth in my own life. Delayed obedience is disobedience, and God's Spirit will only reveal His will to those who are already walking in step with Him. Has He called you to turn from a sin in your life? *Do it.* Has He called you to an act of love toward someone hard to love? *Do it.* Obeying God's Spirit in the clear things opens

---

6. See Matthew 13:12.

our eyes to discern His direction in the hidden things.

We devalue work, so we fail to see the divine in the mundane.

Somewhere along the course of history, we've decided that God only values "sacred work" done in churches or on mission fields; our regular "secular" jobs are to be tolerated because they pay the bills and finance our weekend pleasures (and, of course, the "sacred work" of the church). We grumble about our jobs and complain about our work, seeing it more like a curse than a divine calling.

But God created humans with the distinct privilege of ruling the earth with Him, working on this earth as His representatives, His priests in the world. All work is God's work when it's empowered by and offered to God as an act of worship (see 1 Corinthians 10:31).

When we truly understand the privilege of walking with God in our daily lives, our mundane becomes contoured by the divine.

## Living Lives of Obedient Love

Much of our pop Christianity today focuses on how we feel in our life with Jesus, but Jesus Himself was extremely preoccupied with His followers actually hearing and doing what He commanded.

It's not about how the worship music makes us feel on Sunday morning, but how we live poured-out lives of worship from Monday to Saturday.

It's not about how many verses we can quote to defend our political viewpoints, but how well we embody the Word made flesh to our politically opposite next-door neighbors.

It's not about how pious our prayers sound during Sunday school, but how our hearts hear the whisper of God both in our hidden rooms and in our lived-out interactions with others.

Again and again, Jesus pushes His followers to this gravitational center: "Love one another. As I have loved you, so you must love one another" (John 13:34). This love is not a feeling; it's obedient love in action. After all, "By this everyone will know that you are my disciples, if you love one another" (John 13:35).

When Jesus describes life in His kingdom, He frames His teaching in terms of practical obedience: "Whoever *practices and teaches these commands* will be called great in the kingdom of heaven" and "everyone who hears these words of mine and *puts them into practice* is like a wise man who built his house on the rock" (Matthew 5:19 and 7:24).

Jesus is concerned that His disciples actually *do* what He teaches.

## Remaining in the Love of Jesus Together

In many ways, walking with God is the culmination of all the other Rhythms of Delight. Walking in the light of His presence and obedience to His Spirit is only possible when we're practicing Worship, Word, Whisper, and Wonder. These rhythms do not exist as isolated from each other, but as interwoven movements of God's Spirit in us and through us.

We end with this Rhythm of Walking with God as a reminder that delighting in Jesus has always been greater than just an individual pursuit of joy. God's plan for His people has always been that we would image Him to the world through our love for one another, worked out in practical ways.

Yes, this might look like delivering a plate of scones to a friend in obedience to the prompting of God's Spirit. Or it might look like moving halfway around the world to serve in the hidden places where only God's Spirit knows your work. Most likely, it will look like practicing the presence of God right where you are, faithfully loving Him and loving others in a million little ways.

This is what it means to delight in Jesus; this is what it looks like to remain in His love. It's to be grounded by His loving presence, energized by His Spirit's presence, and motivated by His Father's returning presence to once again dwell with us on earth. We are on mission, not to save the world for God, but to join God in what He is already doing through His Spirit in the world, right where we are.

Small acts of great love are the good works that God prepared for us to walk in, from eternity past and into our eternal future to come. And when we join God in the good work He's doing in the world through His Spirit, He restores our joy step by step as we walk with Him, just like Jesus did.

How do we become women and men who work with such excellence and passion in collaboration with God's Spirit wherever He has called us? What does it look like to keep in step with God's Spirit as He guides and directs us throughout our day?

Let's turn to the example of Jesus to learn from Him how to joyfully walk with God.

# CHAPTER 14

# Practicing Jesus' Rhythm of Walking

On a rainy day a couple years ago, as I was driving home from an appointment, I started thinking about a sweet friend who had recently lost her father. *Show me how to love her, Lord*, I prayed. I was at a loss for how to comfort her.

My rumbling stomach reminded me it was time for lunch, so I found a local bakery off the highway and picked up a panini. On a whim, I ordered a few extra blueberry scones and coffee, deciding to drive a half hour out of my way to take them to my friend. When I arrived, she crushed me in an embrace, and I simply held her tight.

"These are for you," I said, when she finally released me, extending my little offering toward her. She looked at the cardboard box and teared up. *Uh-oh*, I thought. *Did I do something wrong?*

"Did you know," she swiped her tears with the corner of her sleeve, "that I know them?" She tapped the logo on top of the brown pastry box. "They bought our house a few years ago and started their bakery right out of their new home."

My jaw dropped. *Out of all the places in northeast Ohio, how did You lead me there, Lord?*

"I love seeing them grow. It's so special to me." With tears in her eyes, she smiled at me. "How did you know?"

I shrugged, sheepish. "I didn't. But I think God did. He took me there."

## Walking Out Jesus' Love Through Good Works

This small act of kindness was a tangible expression of love for my friend. Yes, it was prompted by my love for her, but ultimately, *it was God's expression of love for her* through me. His way of whispering to her heart: I see you, I know you, and I care for you.

As part of the body of Christ, we move as His hands and feet when we serve one another. We get to embody what Jesus would do for our friends and for strangers, because He's the One energizing us through His Spirit to do these good works. It's like our brain telling our hand to lift a cup of water to quench our thirst—the whole body works together to meet its needs, and our head, that is Jesus, compels us to do acts of kindness that care for the whole body.

And in receiving these acts of kindness, we get to experience Jesus' love for us in tangible ways. A meal dropped off on our doorstep isn't just the thoughtfulness of a friend—we get to receive it as if Jesus Himself were dropping off a meal.

Jesus invites us to participate in His acts of love toward one another, and when we obey His Spirit's prompts and walk out that love, He receives it *as if we are doing it for Him.* Because we are:

"Now you are the body of Christ, and each one of you is a part of it" (1 Corinthians 12:27).[1] We've taken this "body of Christ" language so figuratively that we've forgotten it is, in a very spiritual sense, quite literal.

> We get to serve the invisible Jesus by loving the visible people around us.

Consider these words from Jesus, which He will speak to those who walked out His love in practical ways, like giving a cup of water, clothing the naked, or visiting the imprisoned: "The King will reply, 'Truly I tell you, whatever you did for one of the least of these brothers and sisters of mine, you did for me'" (Matthew 25:40).

That's mind-boggling. We get to serve the invisible Jesus by loving the visible people around us. Think about how small these acts are, these movements of kindness that Jesus points to—even a simple cup of water. Sometimes we're so preoccupied with the desire to do great things for God, we forget He has called us to faithful love in the little things.

And those little things? They add up over time. After all, "God is able to bless you abundantly, so that in all things at all times, having all that you need, *you will abound in every good work*" (2 Corinthians 9:8).

Every act of love is walking with God—when we're doing it out of a place of delighting in Jesus, when we're filled up to over-flowing with God's loving presence, as opposed to, for example, acts of service done out of obligation, manipulation, or a desire for others' acclamation. In other words, when we truly delight in Jesus through the rhythms we've discussed throughout this book, we're so attuned to His Spirit in us, so in step with His pace in the yoke of love, that we don't have to wonder, "Is helping/serving

---

1. See 1 Corinthians 12:12–27.

this person God's will?" We just do it, and sometimes we don't even realize it was God's Spirit leading us into that fruit of love until we look back and see the "coincidences" that are truly His hand at work.

We don't have to strive to come up with ideas on our own for how to show God's love to the world, because God Himself has prepared this work for each of us: "We are God's handiwork, created in Christ Jesus to do good works, *which God prepared in advance for us to do*" (Ephesians 2:10). We just need to walk in step with His Spirit, watching, listening, obeying where He prompts us to love.

## Jesus Walked Obediently to His Father

A few years ago, I was so burned-out from all the good things I was trying to get done every day that I'd collapse in bed overwhelmed by all I had not checked off my list. "There just isn't enough of me to go around," I confided in a friend who had asked how she could pray for me.

> It comforts me to think that when Jesus went to sleep each night, He still left tasks others considered undone; yet He rested in peace, knowing that He had done enough.

"When I feel that way," she responded, "I try to remember that Jesus did only what His Father told Him to do. He didn't heal every sick person; He didn't cast out every demon; He didn't feed every hungry person. There was still work left to be done at the end of every day, but Jesus was never frazzled or overwhelmed. He had learned how to 'do the work that His Father had given Him to do' and nothing more."

That thought has stuck with me these many years, and as I searched the Scriptures, I found them to be true:

**Jesus did only what His Father showed Him to do:**
"Very truly I tell you, the Son can do nothing by himself;
he can do only what he sees his Father doing, because
whatever the Father does the Son also does" (John 5:19).

**Jesus pursued only what His Father willed Him to do:**
"For I have come down from heaven not to do my will but
to do the will of him who sent me" (John 6:38).

**Jesus spoke only what the Father gave Him to say:**
"For I did not speak on my own, but the Father who sent
me commanded me to say all that I have spoken. . . . So
whatever I say is just what the Father has told me to say"
(John 12:49–50).

**Jesus completed only the work the Father gave Him to
finish:** "I have brought you glory on earth by finishing the
work you gave me to do" (John 17:4).

I recently read that when prominent theologian and pastor
Dallas Willard was asked to describe Jesus in one word, his response was "relaxed."[2] Jesus never rushed. He didn't hurry. He
was fully present in each present moment. It comforts me to think
that when Jesus went to sleep each night, He still left tasks others
considered undone; yet He rested in peace, knowing that He had
done enough. For He had done only what the Father gave Him
to do.

---

2. Bill Gaultiere, "A Simple Solution to Stress From Dallas Willard," https://www
.soulshepherding.org/a-simple-solution-to-stress-from-dallas-willard/.

### Decluttering your shoebox with God

Remember that forest walk with my friend Juli? She encouraged me to visualize my life as a shoebox. "There's a limited amount of space in a shoebox," she explained, "but over time we keep adding more to our little box, without taking much out. We just shove it all in, trying to make it all fit even when our box comes apart at the seams."

Here's how to declutter your shoebox with God. Take a couple of hours to "dump out your shoebox" by writing on a piece of paper all your tasks, projects, and responsibilities. Reflect with Jesus: *What does it feel like to write it all down?*

Set aside your figurative shoebox for a few days, asking God for wisdom. Then bring each item before Jesus and ask: *Does this go back into my shoebox?* As you prayerfully consider each item, ask God for strength to let go of things that are past their time.

On a separate sheet of paper, draw a new "shoebox" and add only those things that God wants you to carry into the next season of your life. As you do, you may sense God's peace settling in your heart, knowing that these few priorities come from Him. Everything else can be paused.

When I consulted with my husband and a few trusted mentors, they each confirmed I needed to slow down and strip back to the bare essentials I'd returned to my shoebox following my walk with Juli. God worked to heal me in the year that followed—physically, spiritually, mentally, and emotionally—restoring my joy a little more each day.

### Praying over your calendar

My shoebox feels lighter these days, but I still feel overwhelmed sometimes. Thinking back on Jesus' example, I pause to pray, "Father, what have *You* given *me* to do today?"

You may find it helpful to literally open your task list or calendar and pray over each item. *Show me, Lord, which of these things come from You, and which of them are my own ambition or other people's misplaced demands.*

Whenever I pray over my agenda this way, God's Spirit never fails to simplify my tasks and prioritize my time. Remember that Jesus' yoke is easy, His burden is light, and His pace is never rushed.

Occasionally, this means reevaluating my commitments or my family's activities. When I find there's little margin in our schedule, it means I'm driven by something other than God's Spirit. Together with my husband, we prayerfully reevaluate which things we're still doing because "we've always done them" or because our friends are doing them, but they're not what God is calling our family to do. This includes extracurricular activities, church volunteering, ministry opportunities, standing commitments, and even job responsibilities. We put it all on paper and bring it before the Lord: "What are You giving us to do in this season, Lord?"

Then we excuse ourselves from what's past its time and recommit ourselves to walk in obedience to those things God has given us to do.

### Planned acts of love and obedience

Sometimes we have every intention of obeying God, but life just kind of gets in the way. We've felt God's tug to call that friend and check on her, or we've sensed that He wants us to help rake our neighbor's yard, but life gets busy, we put it off, and pretty soon, we forget He'd even whispered anything in the first place.

One practice that has brought me much joy over the years has been planning acts of love with God's own Spirit. After I've reviewed my weekly schedule in prayer and asked God to help me prioritize what *He would have me do*, I whisper one more prayer:

"Who are You calling me to serve this week?" It's like I'm giving God permission (as if He needs it) to add secret acts of loving-kindness to my week. If you've never tried, I highly recommend it. It's a blast to feel like you're conspiring with the Creator of the universe to bless people when they're least expecting it.

Sometimes, in response, God's Spirit reminds me of an act of love He had already placed on my heart. In my experience, He usually won't reveal any new projects for us to walk in together until I take the next step to obey what He's already shown me to do. Sometimes, He calls me to repentance, showing me an area of my life where He really wants to grow me, or He's calling me to increased surrender. In that case, there's no room to move outward in service until He's brought healing and restoration to my own heart.

But every time I take the next step in obedience to God's Spirit leading me, it's the most exhilarating feeling—sometimes scary, especially when He takes me outside of my comfort zone; sometimes freeing, like when He leads me to face one of my fears with Him; but always joy, walking in step with Him, doing what He shows me to do.

### Letting go of unfinished tasks

Saying yes to God's spontaneous prompts means that sometimes other things don't get done. This used to weigh heavily on me, and sometimes it still does.

One simple habit that has helped me at the end of my day has been to release those unfinished tasks to Jesus. I picture myself handing over my to-do lists—some tasks completed, many others unfinished—and asking Him to hold on to it overnight. *I guess they weren't that important*, I whisper in prayer. *Help me leave them with You as I go to sleep tonight.*

## Confessing our shortcomings; receiving more grace

But sometimes I don't finish my work because I allowed myself to get distracted by "shiny objects" that felt more exciting than the work God had given me to do. Sometimes I look back and see all the ways I failed to show Jesus' love, all the ways I failed to walk in obedience.

In those evening reviews with Jesus, His Spirit may convict me that I wasted time on social media, mindlessly scrolling instead of purposefully engaging. Or maybe He reminds me that I stayed up late lost in a book instead of going to sleep at a reasonable hour, which meant I woke up tired and lacking energy, which derailed my whole day.

Over the years, I've learned that the Spirit's voice of conviction is *tender and compassionate*. When He convicts me of sin, He always guides me toward repentance, turning me toward the embrace of my heavenly Father, and moving to restore my joy. In contrast, the voice of the accuser carries condemnation and guilt. When he flings failure in my face, he always urges me to turn away from God in shame, to hide myself from His face, like he did with Adam and Eve and every human being since.

When Satan tempts me to despair, I remember that Jesus stands as our Great High Priest who intercedes for us, who offers His righteousness in place of our sins, and who is "faithful and just and will forgive us our sins and purify us from all unrighteousness" (1 John 1:9). Let us be quick to confess our sins and experience the joy of Jesus' perfect love and forgiveness even in our places of failure.

Nothing can separate us from the great love of God extended toward us in Christ Jesus. Even our failures become avenues to experience His wonderful restoration toward joy. And the more we walk with God, the more faithfully we stay close to His side in all our work.

## Jesus Walked Faithfully in All His Work

Because the gospel narratives focus primarily on Jesus' three years of public ministry, we seem to forget that He spent most of His years in hidden faithfulness:

- As a child, Jesus obeyed His parents and "grew in wisdom and stature, and in favor with God and man" (Luke 2:52). His Nazarene neighbors didn't recognize the glory of God within Him, but they approved of His behavior within their village during the first thirty years of His life. As a faithful Jew, Jesus would have observed all the Torah commands to love God and love His neighbors as Himself.

- As a carpenter, Jesus worked faithfully in His day job, crafting items from wood or stone, and possibly working as a contractor on Herod's many building projects.[3] This work was not insignificant to Jesus—He'd have spent nearly twenty years laboring with His hands.

- As a rabbi, Jesus poured out His love every hour of His day, not just during His teaching moments or miraculous events. Jesus lived out faithful love when He stopped for a drink at a well (John 4:5–30) and when He turned to the woman who touched His robe (Mark 5:22–43) and during every other interruption to His "scheduled" ministry.

---

3. As a Jewish boy who did not become a rabbi's disciple, Jesus would have apprenticed with his earthly father, Joseph the carpenter, and was later known as a carpenter Himself. But the Greek word used to describe His work can refer to a broader range of manual labor, including "artisan," "contractor," or "handyman," and there's evidence to suggest that Jesus may have worked on Herod's many building projects, perhaps even the temple in Jerusalem. Blue Letter Bible, "Blue Letter Bible Dictionary Entries, *carpenter*," https://www.blueletterbible.org/search/Dictionary/viewTopic.cfm?topic=ET0000727,IT0001879,VT0000413,BT0000889.

- As our Savior, Jesus "learned obedience from what he suffered" (Hebrews 5:8) and "being found in appearance as a man, he humbled himself by becoming obedient to death—even death on a cross!" (Philippians 2:8).

We have much to learn from Jesus here, and it's super practical in lots of ways.

### Undistracted attention

We don't know what kind of a playmate Jesus was to His village friends, but it's not hard to imagine that He was the kind of friend who gave someone His undivided attention.

You know the kind of person I'm describing, right?

It's the person who is so focused on the one they're talking to, that everything else seems to fade in the background. The person in front of them becomes their singular focus, the most important thing in that moment. Their focused gaze can feel unnerving at first, so accustomed are we to distracted conversation partners; but spend time with such a person, and you'll find their gaze communicates infinite value and worth.

That's how Jesus looked at people: with a gaze of eternal love (see Mark 10:21).

As we learn to keep in step with Jesus, He calls us to slow down and give each person we encounter our undivided attention. I'll admit, this is hard for me, but I've learned to ask Him to help me—*Help me see this person as You see them, Jesus. Help me to listen to them as You would listen to them. Help me to love them like You love them.* This means resisting the temptation to check my phone or look around the room when someone's talking to me. It means giving the person in front of me my full, undistracted attention.

Sometimes, when I'm in conversation with another, I silently ask

God's Spirit to help me perceive what's going on beneath the surface. *What do You want to show me, God? Help me discern what You would have me say to them here.* Sometimes, there's nothing other than small talk, and I practice love by doing my best to stay engaged as we talk about the weather or their kids' sports schedule. But other times, God's Spirit quickens my spiritual senses to pick up on subtle hints that then fuel my prayers for that person, and often lead to practical ways I can show them the love of Jesus in the coming days.

A habit of undistracted attention also means that when my children walk into a room to talk to me, I want to put down my phone and physically turn my body to face them. When my husband is telling me about his day, I need to stop my scroll and listen with my full self. It also means turning off notifications on all my apps so that they don't pull me from the people in front of me.

And sometimes it means putting my phone on "do not disturb" so that outside interruptions don't steal my attention from family meals or times of worship or a deep conversation.

I want to represent Jesus to the people in front of me. I want them to feel the love of Jesus in my gaze, the comfort of Jesus in my touch, the presence of Jesus in my attention, even when they interrupt me.

### A ministry of interruptions

Any parent knows how frustrating it is to be interrupted in the middle of an "important task" in order to deal with something our little ones deem urgent. And any one of us who has worked a day job knows what it's like to be interrupted by a coworker too. But what if we asked God to help us see these interruptions as He does?

The gospel of Mark records thirty-five times Jesus was interrupted. And each time, He made time for them. No task was more important than the person right in front of Him.

I tend to plan my days with very little margin, much to my chagrin, and any interruption threatens to get me off track. I've got a schedule that serves as my GPS; but what if these detours are the very path Jesus wants us to walk together?

When I find myself frustrated by interruptions, I try to pause, take a deep breath, and picture myself looking over to Jesus, the two of us in a yoke.

I'm not great at embracing interruptions, but as I'm slowing my pace to walk in step with Jesus, I'm learning that it's often in those interruptions that He has most to teach me. "Learn from me," He whispers.

*I guess we're pausing here?* Deep breath. *Okay Jesus, help me see what You see. Help me do what You do. Show me the work You have for me here.*

And when I look back on my day as I lie in bed, it's often in those interruptions that I witness God doing His most powerful work.

### Serving God in our "secular" work

As we've already seen, there is no secular or sacred divide with God, so all our work is holy to Him. Jesus Himself faithfully worked as a carpenter for decades. But many of us have been conditioned to think that the "Christian way" to do our work is to leave gospel tracts in the bathroom or veer conversations uncomfortably toward spiritual topics.

Reflecting on a conversation with a church member about how to work his day job as a Christian, Pastor Tim Keller responds, "What is the Christian way to fly a plane? I'll tell you what the Christian way is to fly that plane—land. If you are really good, land the plane so it can take off again." This amusing quip illustrates that faithfulness in our daily work is what it means to "work unto the Lord" (see Colossians 3:23–24).

As a teenager, I kept a notebook filled with quotes I wanted to remember from my reading, and I revisited them often. Recently, I reread this quote from Martin Luther King Jr. that shaped how I viewed my first jobs as a young adult:

> If a man is called to be a street sweeper, he should sweep streets even as Michelangelo painted, or Beethoven composed music, or Shakespeare wrote poetry. He should sweep streets so well that all hosts of heaven and earth pause to say: "Here lives a great sweeper who did his job well."[4]

My very first paid job as a ten-year-old was painting ceramic pottery. Then I worked as a kitchen helper at a summer camp, a banquet server in my college dining hall, and a translator of written curriculum for a church.

In my early twenties, I worked as a writing tutor, a library assistant, a public relations intern, a data entry clerk, and a telemarketer. (Yep, I worked in a call center. I was one of *those people* because I needed to pay my bills.) In each of those positions, King's words resounded in my subconscious and formed the prayer of my working hours: "Here lives a dishwasher/server/telemarketer, who does her job well."

Whatever you consider your "job," what would it look like to work at it faithfully—*joyfully even*—as if you were serving Jesus? Picture yourself flipping a burger and serving it to Jesus. Does that thought make you smile like it does me? Picture answering a phone call (or more dreadfully, *making a telemarketing call*) as if

---

4. Martin Luther King Jr., "The Drum Major Instinct," speech delivered at the Ebenezer Baptist Church, Atlanta, Georgia, February 4, 1968, in *A Knock at Midnight: Inspiration from the Great Sermons of Reverend Martin Luther King, Jr.* (New York: Warner Books, 1998), 126.

Jesus was on the other side of the line. What would that conversation sound like?

Delighting in Jesus means bringing an awareness of His presence with us into our regular work. We don't have to escape to a convent or a church to experience the thrill of His presence; we just need to faithfully show up and do the work as for Him, rooted in love and pouring out love, to hear His whisper, "Well done, good and faithful servant" (Matthew 25:23).

### Practicing the presence of God

Four centuries ago, a French man injured in war and living in poverty devoted himself to a life of service in a Parisian convent. Brother Lawrence started his tenure as a lay brother by working in the kitchen and, in his later years, repairing sandals.

At first, he was frustrated by his menial tasks, thinking he'd rather devote his hours to prayer like the monks; but in time, he discovered the joy of doing all his work with an awareness of God's loving presence:

> We ought not to be weary of *doing little things for the love of God*, who regards not the greatness of the work, but the love with which it is performed. . . . We need only to recognize GOD intimately present with us, to address ourselves to Him every moment, that we may beg His assistance for knowing His will in things doubtful, and for rightly performing those which we plainly see He requires of us, *offering them to Him before we do them*, and giving Him thanks when we have done.[5]

---

5. Brother Lawrence, *The Practice of the Presence of God*. Kindle. Emphasis added.

Like Brother Lawrence, I'm often tempted to rush through boring tasks to get on to "the more important work" that excites me. But what would it look like for us to slow down and become aware of God's presence with us *during* those boring tasks? To offer them to Him as we do them, *This is for You, Jesus.*

Such a simple practice can transform how we go about our days, no longer rushing to the big things, but doing even "the little things for the love of God."

## How Will You Delight in Obedience to God?

Do you see how exciting it is to walk with God, to partner with Him in the work He is doing in the world? We don't need to move to a different country to serve Jesus. As my college adviser said to me when I was trying to pick a major: "People with needs are everywhere. Be faithful to serve wherever God has placed you, and let Him do the rest."

God invites us to delight in Him as we walk in step with His Spirit, living lives of poured-out love. And as we learn to walk in rhythm with Him, we'll experience the joy of seeing Him do "mighty things" in our ordinary lives.

**Take some time now to review the practical habits shared in this chapter, or come up with one of your own. What would it look like for you to walk with God in the next month?**

- How will you make this Rhythm of Walking with God small?

- What daily routines can you link to your walking? "When I _____, I will _____."

- How can you make your Rhythm of Walking fun and personal to you?

- How will you celebrate your growth each week? Month? Year?

Like all the other rhythms of delighting in Jesus, this one may take time to become a regular part of your life. But remember that we practice these habits not to garner spiritual favor with God or manipulate His will to match our wishes. We walk in step with our friend Jesus because we want to abide in His love, dwell in His presence, and move in response to His whispers. And as we walk with Him, we'll see His kingdom come, His will be done, on earth—in our lives, in our homes, and in our communities—as it is in heaven. May His reign start here, now, with us. Amen.

PART THREE

# Our Joy Fulfilled

# CHAPTER 15

# This Is Our Happily Ever After

A few weeks ago, I ran into the grocery store to grab a few items for dinner.

Rushing through the aisles, I spotted someone who looked vaguely familiar in the bread aisle, but I couldn't quite place her face. Curious, part of me wanted to say hello, but I moved on to avoid an awkward interaction, since I couldn't remember her name. I've had enough embarrassing social encounters to last a lifetime.

But when I got to the self-checkout lane, the only spot open was right next to this woman. I casually looked over through the corner of my eye while scanning the milk gallon and clamshell strawberries, hoping I didn't look like a creep.

*Beep. Beep.*

With each item scanned, I hoped my brain would find the correct entry in my mental registrar, maybe somewhere among the "J" names, but it came up blank. *I wish I had that superpower where*

*I remembered everyone's name,* I thought for the thousandth time. *She really looks like that lady from our prayer group years ago.*

As I reached for my last item in the cart, I glanced up under my lashes for one last look. Our eyes connected.

"Asheritah? I thought that was you." Her gorgeous smile lit up her face. "I'd recognize those sparkling eyes any day!"

I nearly dropped the carton of eggs I was holding. *Lord, did she just say "sparkling eyes"?* I pondered the coincidence.

Jeanette was kind enough to remind me of her name, and we embraced right there between the checkout counters, promising to meet up for coffee soon. A few minutes later, walking back to my car, I mentally replayed the encounter again and again.

*You did it, Jesus,* I marveled. *You really did it.*

Nearly eighteen months after that desperate scribbled prayer in the conference room, Jesus had restored the sparkle to my eyes. And He'd set me up in this unexpected grocery store encounter to prove it.

*Only You, Jesus,* I smiled as I drove home. *Only You could restore the sparkle to my eyes, and I'll forever praise You!* My heart echoed the conclusion of Psalm 13:

> But I trust in your unfailing love.
> > I will rejoice because you have rescued me.
> I will sing to the LORD
> > because he is good to me.[1]

Jesus had walked me through the mountains and the valleys, and I lived to tell about it.

---

1. See Psalm 13:5–6.

# He Makes Everything Beautiful in His Time

Reflecting on the past decade of my life, I can see how God has patiently guided me, how He has lovingly grown me, how He has tenderly healed me through these Rhythms of Delight. This journey has not been linear; more like a cyclical progression—like the sun rising and setting but always moving time forward. Each cyclical movement through these rhythms takes us deeper and deeper in every season with Jesus until the day we finally meet Him face-to-face.

I can look back now and see how far God has brought me, how He restores the years that the locusts had eaten. How He turns evil into good. How He is making everything beautiful in His time.[2]

This is the part where you'd expect me to reveal that my father and I have reconciled, and our relationship is stronger than before. But real life doesn't work out like a Hollywood movie. God doesn't give us the script beforehand, warning us about the conflict to come or reassuring us that all the characters make up in the end.

We're not the hero of this story. The hero is our faithful Jesus who is preparing His bride for the day He returns to take her home. Yes, He is bringing His kingdom here on earth, and He's already started, but there's still much to be done.

You see, we live in the tension of *already, but not yet*. He has started the work already, and He will be faithful to complete it; in the meantime, we're in the "not yet," learning to *lean into Him*—to delight our hearts in Him—as He shapes our desires and affections for eternity.[3] We learn to *Walk* with Him, to *Wonder* at Him, to *Whisper* with Him, to open His *Word* with Him, and to *Worship*

---

2. See Joel 2:25–29; Genesis 50:20; Ecclesiastes 3:11.

3. See Philippians 1:6; Psalm 37:4; Proverbs 3:5–6.

Him. Our hearts yearn for Him until the day we finally see Him face-to-face.

And when we've finally reached the end, whether through death or through His return, we'll discover that all our earthly lives were but preparation for the rest of eternity.

As C. S. Lewis describes in the last book of the Chronicles of Narnia series:

> All their life in this world and all their adventures in Narnia had only been the cover and the title page: now at last they were beginning Chapter One of the Great Story which no one on earth has read: which goes on forever: in which every chapter is better than the one before.[4]

We cannot even fathom how glorious a future awaits us with Jesus, how beautiful our reunion with Him will be when all our longings finally find their fulfillment in Him. As the Bible says, "the things God has prepared for those who love him" are so indescribable that they're "what no eye has seen, what no ear has heard, and what no human mind has conceived" (1 Corinthians 2:9).

And we're not talking about the streets of gold or gem-studded buildings here. The treasure of our eternity in heaven is Jesus Himself, the mysterious union foreshadowed by every epic love story.

**We cannot even fathom how glorious a future awaits us with Jesus, how beautiful our reunion with Him will be when all our longings finally find their fulfillment in Him.**

---

4. C. S. Lewis, *The Last Battle* (New York: Scholastic, 1995), Kindle, 121.

# Our Joy Fulfilled

One of my guilty pleasures is scrolling through clips on Instagram that feature a couple's first look on their wedding day. The tears come unbidden as I take in the groom's sheer delight upon seeing his radiant fiancée in her bridal gown.

That first look communicates a world of emotions: admiration, longing, affection, passion, desire. Sometimes you can see each emotion play across a groom's features as he admires his bride before pulling her into an embrace.

I think back on my own wedding day, then back to the start of my relationship with Flaviu, my junior high nemesis who became my high school crush until we started dating long-distance halfway through my freshman year of college.

We were separated by an ocean: I attended college in Ohio and he in Romania. As hard as it is for our children to imagine, our relationship started long before FaceTime, and long-distance phone calls were too expensive for two poor college students. We coordinated our schedules to the seven-hour time difference, and every afternoon found me sitting with my laptop in the student center, typing away in a tiny box at the corner of my screen.

I tried to "hear" Flaviu's voice as I read his instant messages, and I became a much faster typer during the hundreds of hours we messaged back and forth, into the wee hours of his morning.

I was grateful for the daily connection, but no joy compared to the sweet reunion of seeing him face-to-face several months later, hearing his actual voice whisper sweet nothings in my ear, feeling his arms wrap around me. He joined me on campus the following fall, and we've been inseparable ever since. Our first bridal look is not documented on film, but it's forever seared in my memory, when Flaviu scooped me into his arms and swung me around in circles.

Flaviu has been God's best gift to me, apart from Jesus. Through the darkest seasons of my life, my husband's presence has often embodied Jesus' care for me, and God has brought deep healing to my soul through my husband's faithful love. Our marriage, imperfect as it may be, has foreshadowed the glorious union that awaits us with Jesus.

## Your Wedding Invitation: Come!

I'm not overly romanticizing our individual relationship with Jesus, as we are corporately His bride and not some bizarre harem of wives. But there certainly is truth to the imagery of a bride and her groom, a long-distance relationship that's finally satisfied in that first look, that wedding ceremony, that beginning of a happily ever after.

Jesus spoke about marriage suppers in Matthew 22:1–14 and 25:1–13, and Paul explained how human marriages image the spiritual marriage between Jesus and His bride in Ephesians 5:31–32. Then in Revelation 19:6–9, we get a preview of the wedding to come:

> Then I heard what sounded like a great multitude, like the roar of rushing waters and like loud peals of thunder, shouting:
>
> "Hallelujah!
>  For our Lord God Almighty reigns.
> *Let us rejoice and be glad*
>  *and give him glory!*
> *For the wedding of the Lamb has come,*
>  *and his bride has made herself ready.*
> Fine linen, bright and clean,
>  was given her to wear."

(Fine linen stands for the righteous acts of God's holy people.)
Then the angel said to me, "Write this: Blessed are those who
are invited to *the wedding supper of the Lamb!*" And he added,
"These are the true words of God."

Our wedding day is coming, and though we've never seen Jesus, our hearts know Him well. These rhythms teach our souls to delight in Him from afar, though He's lovingly placed His own Spirit in us. Soon we'll finally get to see Him face-to-face, to hear His voice, to know the joy of His embrace. And all these years we've spent here on earth getting to know Him, delighting in Him, collaborating with Him will seem like a blink of the eye when we get our first look, and our joy will finally be fulfilled.

What a glorious day that will be!

Until then, Jesus' Spirit invites us to come and join the party:

The Spirit and the bride say, "Come!"
And let the one who hears say, "Come!"
Let the one who is thirsty come;
and let the one who wishes take the free gift of the water of life.
(Revelation 22:17)

So come, dear one. Find your joy in Jesus, the One who delights in you, until we finally see His face, and feel His embrace, and enjoy Him for all eternity.

# Acknowledgments

E very book bears the fingerprints of countless people behind the scenes whose love and whose lives made it possible. Never has that been more true for me than with this book you're holding in your hands. *Delighting in Jesus* is a message years in the making, perhaps even my whole life long, and a proper acknowledgment of the people who've joined me on this journey would fill another book. I'll try to keep this short.

To my Moody team who believed in this book and brought this dream to life: Judy, Amanda, Ashley, Hope, Trillia, Randall, Steve, and so many others. Each book is a thrilling ride, and I couldn't have asked for better partners in publishing. Thank you.

To Ann Kroeker: I doubt this book would have seen the light of day had you not tenderly shepherded me through those early discombobulated drafts and through the arduous cuts, cuts, cuts! My readers and I both thank you!

To my writing friends who have become really dear friends: Wendy, Niki, Renee, Rachel, Kim, Jenni. Thank you for praying me into this, through this, and all the way out of it too. Let's plan more writing retreats, okay?

To Carol, Linda, Juli, Sally, Carmen, Silvia, Simona, and many other mothers in the faith who have mentored me through your writing and your very lives: *thank you.*

To my hilariously funny friends Melissa and Hannah: for literally walking with me through the dark valleys and into the sunshine again. I know we're in for a riotous good time when I'm with either of you. You've been the hands and feet and smiles of Jesus to me. Thank you.

To Kate, Bethany, Ana, Amanda, Laura, Jen, Ashley, Emily, Julie, Jennifer, Jamie, Jeanette, Susie, and countless other women who have practiced these rhythms with me in real life in our local church: I've learned so much from each of you. Thank you.

To Dr. Mike: you taught me how to cry. I can't tell you how many times God's Spirit spoke discernment through you. Thank you for talking me through the unspeakable.

To Katrina: you responded to an email of desperation and helped me see this healing journey holistically. Thank you for walking me back to joy.

To Pastor Mike: your theological review makes for the best conversations, but it's your humble leadership that keeps pointing me to Jesus. Thank you.

To Kathryn: God knew I needed you, and He brought you like a spring breeze, promising hope, healing, and a bright future. I continue to marvel at the gift you are in my life and in our ministry. Thank you, friend.

To Eugen and Eli: my story is inextricably bound up in yours. For all your brotherly love over the years, thank you.

To Mom: words fail to capture the many ways your love, prayers, and faith are woven into these pages. Thank you. You stand for our family as a testimony to God's kindness, His faithfulness, and His tender mercy. Truly, He makes everything beautiful in its time.

To Carissa, Amelia, and Theo: being your mom is the grandest adventure of my life—and the most humbling one too. Thank you for all the cuddles, all the kisses, all the prayers, and all the extra grace in this writing season. Now we can bake cookies!

To Frumosul Meu: you embody the love and delight of Jesus to me like no one else. In my darkest, you stood near and loved me out of my fears. Everyone should have a Flaviu in their lives, but you'll forever be mine. *Te iubesc!*

To my precious Jesus: your goodness and mercy have chased me down, your loving-kindness has held me close, and your delight lights up my soul. I can't wait to see you! Come quickly, beloved Jesus. Come.

# We help women enjoy time with Jesus every day

Discover simple ways to find joy in Jesus through creative and consistent Bible habits.

Start Today:

**delightinginjesus.com**

# Delight throughout the year with Asheritah's seasonal devotionals

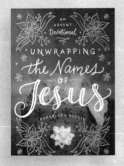

### UNWRAPPING THE NAMES OF JESUS: AN ADVENT DEVOTIONAL

*Unwrapping the Names of Jesus* leads readers through the four weeks of Advent (Hope, Preparation, Joy, and Love) by focusing each day's reflection on one name of Jesus. Each week begins with an interactive family devotional followed by five daily reflections, as well as suggestions for fun-filled family activities or service projects to enhance a family's Advent experience.

### UNWRAPPING THE NAMES OF JESUS FOR KIDS

A captivating story of how a mother encountered Jesus—and His beautiful names—as a little girl. You'll experience Jesus as a real person who meets our real needs. Foster a heart of adoration with this engaging and theologically rich story. Linger over the whimsical illustrations. Wonder and worship together.

### UNCOVERING THE LOVE OF JESUS: A LENT DEVOTIONAL

Reclaim the Lenten season with 40 devotionals that reveal the deep love of Jesus poured out for us. Each daily reflection looks at Jesus' personal interactions in Scripture and leads you in meditation on a new aspect of His love. Don't let Easter pass you by this year.

# More by Asheritah

### PRAYERS OF REST: DAILY PROMPTS TO SLOW DOWN AND HEAR GOD'S VOICE

Asheritah offers you a respite from your spiritual to-do list. She provides guided prayers that will focus your mind and heart on Scripture. Using a memorable acronym and daily Bible verses, this prayer devotional will guide you through worship, confession, stillness, and surrender.

### HE IS ENOUGH: LIVING IN THE FULLNESS OF JESUS – A STUDY IN COLOSSIANS

In this 6-week study of Colossians, Asheritah leads readers to discover the life-altering importance of Jesus' sufficiency and sovereignty. With short meditations for busy days, dig-deep study for days you want more, and supplemental service challenges for leaders, you can study the way that helps you the most.

### BIBLE AND BREAKFAST: 31 MORNINGS WITH JESUS–FEEDING OUR BODIES AND SOULS TOGETHER

Kickstart a morning habit of meeting with Jesus *and* eating a healthy breakfast every day. Join Asheritah for 31 devotions for busy women and 31 breakfast recipes that are healthy enough for you to feel good about and tasty enough that your kids will eat them.

### FULL: FOOD, JESUS, AND THE BATTLE FOR SATISFACTION

Whether the struggle is with excess weight, unwanted cravings, total control, or extreme diets, we all have a relationship with food. *Full* unpacks a theology of food to break its power, help us engage food holistically, and free us to taste and see that God is good.